Surviving Maggie

Surviving Maggie

An Australian Story

JOHN FINGLETON

HarperCollinsPublishers

HarperCollins*Publishers*

First published in Australia in 2011
by HarperCollins*Publishers* Australia Pty Limited
ABN 36 009 913 517
harpercollins.com.au

Copyright © John Fingleton 2011

The right of John Fingleton to be identified as the author of this work
has been asserted by him under the *Copyright Amendment (Moral Rights) Act 2000*.

This work is copyright.
Apart from any use as permitted under the *Copyright Act 1968*, no part may
be reproduced, copied, scanned, stored in a retrieval system, recorded, or transmitted,
in any form or by any means, without the prior written permission of the publisher.

HarperCollins*Publishers*
Level 13, 201 Elizabeth Street, Sydney NSW 2000, Australia
31 View Road, Glenfield, Auckland 0627, New Zealand
A 53, Sector 57, Noida, UP, India
77–85 Fulham Palace Road, London, W6 8JB, United Kingdom
2 Bloor Street East, 20th floor, Toronto, Ontario M4W 1A8, Canada
10 East 53rd Street, New York NY 10022, USA

National Library of Australia Cataloguing-in-Publication entry (pbk)

Fingleton, John.
　　Surviving Maggie / John Fingleton.
　　ISBN: 978 0 7322 9359 8 (pbk.)
　　Fingleton, Harold—Childhood and youth.
　　Fathers—Australia—Biography.
　　Families—Australia—Biography.
　　Abused children—Australia—Biography.
　　Children—Institutional care—Australia—Biography.
306.8742092

Cover design by Christa Moffitt, Christabella Designs
Cover image by Andrew Davis /Trevillion Images
Typeset in Minion 13/19.5pt by Letter Spaced
Printed and bound in Australia by Griffin Press
60gsm Hi Bulk Book Cream used by HarperCollins*Publishers* is a natural, recyclable product made
from wood grown in sustainable forests. The manufacturing processes conform to the
environmental regulations in the country of origin, Finland.

5　4　3　2　1　　11　12　13　14

For dear Sylvia
And for Harold Jnr, Tony, Ronald and Diane

Contents

Foreword   *ix*

Introduction   *1*

1 Captured   5
2 Off to St Vincent's   27
3 Welcome!   33
4 Bloody Mass   41
5 Crime and Punishment   53
6 Getting to Know Tom   61
7 Telling Maggie   71
8 School Days   79
9 Visiting the General   93
10 A Brief Release   103
11 Out for Good   111
12 No More Pencils, No More Books   123
13 Oats for Goats   133
14 Clarrie   149
15 Shortened Up!   163
16 A Little Discretion   169
17 The Country Life   179
18 Ravished   185
19 The Big Smoke   197
20 The Proposal   211

21 Turning Mugs into Men	229
22 The Tomato Fight	243
23 The Betrayal	259
24 Little Fishes	273
In Conclusion	*277*
About the Author	*291*
Acknowledgements	*293*

Foreword

I loved my father simply and unconditionally, because he was my dad. However, I did not fully understand the man or even know much about him, his early life or the troubled upbringing that he endured.

My memories had been clouded by my tendency as a child to avoid any disruption by disappearing or drifting off into my own little world.

My brother John has enabled me to piece together some of those lost times and memories with this book.

John has endeavoured to show our dad as he was – his youth and childhood and the circumstances that conspired to make him the individual he grew to be – not as you may have seen him portrayed in *Swimming Upstream*, Russell Mulcahy's movie about our family. He was a man with many flaws but also a man with great strengths, not the least being his love for his family.

John would ring me after completing every chapter. He would read what he had written and we would discuss it. It proved to be wonderful therapy for us both. His thorough research involved finding out what it was really like in the early years of the twentieth century, especially for a wild young lad from Fortitude Valley.

Our father would have been proud of this book, I am sure, written as it is by the one he loved the most.

Ronald Graham Fingleton

Introduction

A few months prior to the release of *Swimming Upstream*, I had a discussion with my brother Tony, the co-author and co-producer of the film, about what I considered were some inherent inaccuracies in its content and, to my mind, the unfair depiction of our father, Harold Fingleton senior.

'Write your own book if you're not happy,' he challenged me. At that time, I'm sure neither of us suspected that I might take up the challenge. I'd never written more than the occasional essay before. The idea that I might give it a go germinated over the ensuing couple of years and has now borne fruit.

I purposefully conclude this story at the point where the film and the subsequent book of the film begin, mainly to avoid traversing old ground. Bearing in mind the fact that Tony's and my recollection of certain details is vastly different, I also wish not to appear argumentative.

The aim of this book is not to make excuses for my father, because I realise as well as anyone that he was far from perfect. It is to explore the circumstances of his developing years – the experiences that befell him and those he brought upon himself – that produced this most complex of men.

This is the truth as I see it, based on what I have discovered through systematic research, which included accessing police reports from as far back as 1915 and government records now made available to family members by virtue of the extremely sensible freedom-of-information laws. I was also assisted by family, including my Aunt Mollie, who outlived her youngest brother, Harold; old friends of my parents; and, of course, my mother, who supplied me with a huge slice of inside information before she passed away.

In October 1988, when Mum was diagnosed with terminal cancer, there seemed to be but two options available to her: either to be placed in a nursing home or be looked after at home by a nurse. She didn't like the nurse option and the other was definitely out. My sister, Diane, and I decided that between us we could do the job. So with my wife Sylvia's blessing, I went to Brisbane from Sydney, where we live, prepared to stay for as long as it took. Di and I shared the responsibility of seeing Mum through to the end in the place she would be most at peace, her own flat. The few months we spent at Mum's side as she gradually slipped away were sometimes awful and harrowing, yet rewarding. How often does one get the chance to return some love in this way?

When she felt up to it, Mum and I passed the time simply chatting. She knew more than anyone the depth of the compassion I'd always felt for my father and I think she considered me to be more broadminded than the rest of the

Introduction

family, so she was open and honest about some of the more unpleasant secrets of his life and hers that I'd always wanted so desperately to know about.

This is not a happy story for the most part but it is one that I am proud to relate. There are some isolated instances where, by necessity, I have had to use common sense and my intimate knowledge of the main characters to describe scenes and conversations and to tell the story as completely as possible. In some cases, it was necessary for me to create names for people.

However, there is no embellishment or exaggeration of the most important details of this stark tale. All the anecdotes are based on facts that I gathered during my research and discussions with family members.

If I were asked to use one word to best describe my father, Harold Fingleton, that word would be 'enigmatic'. He was a man of almost dual personalities: occasionally talkative, jovial and sociable; capable of the most touching gentleness, with young children especially; at other times desperately sad, inward-looking and non-communicative. He could demonstrate the most incredible strength of character and yet his vulnerability and his weaknesses were apparent for all to see. Typically for a man of his times, his opinions and his loyalties were rigid and beyond challenge or debate, yet he recognised all too well what he saw as his place in the scheme of things. With the determined assistance and guidance of our mother, Dora, he set about providing his family with the best possible opportunities to break down the very walls that he himself constructed, yet he never sought to venture beyond those walls himself.

I am under no illusions as to the worth of my writing but I have endeavoured to narrate my father's tale with honesty. It is, ultimately, Harold's story, the story of one whom I loved with all of my heart.

1
Captured

*When we are born, we cry that we are come
To this great stage of fools*

Lear, *King Lear*, William Shakespeare (1564–1616)

Patrick could dance you a jig. He could sing you a sweet, sad song or a stirring one, tell a yarn to bring a tear to the eye, fight and beat the best man in the bar or drink him dizzy. In short, Patrick was an Irishman – and a happy one. In fact, if you asked Pat if he was happy, he'd tell you straight, in the broadest of brogues, that 'never a happier man breathed air'.

He was handsome, tall, lean and strong, with the shock of thick, straight, dark hair that the Fingleton stock had been blessed with through the generations. His decision to leave his home and the cold, damp poverty of the village of Stradbally in 1882 and travel across the world to Australia, working as a ship's carpenter to pay for his berth, had been well taken. It brought changes to his life the likes of which he could never have imagined. He'd arrived in Sydney on his twentieth birthday and immediately headed north in search of the subtropical warmth of Queensland. He quickly found work as a carpenter, played any sport he could get involved in and lived a carefree existence. Early in 1889, he met the charming and pretty Margaret Daunt, who'd been living in Brisbane since she was three years old. Her parents were Irish but she'd been born in Liverpool, England, in 1862, the same year as Patrick. They married on 18 August 1889 and looked forward to starting a family as quickly as possible.

Maggie experienced no trouble in falling pregnant and their firstborn, Mary Elizabeth, arrived on 24 June 1890. Patrick nicknamed her Mollie, after his favourite sister, and she carried that name for her entire life.

By January 1909, when their youngest son, Harold William, was born, they'd had another five children. Margaret Julia was born in 1892, Peter Paul in 1897, Kathleen Delores (Kitty) in 1900, Patrick Joseph in 1903 and Ellen Veronica (Nellie) in 1905.

Maggie's life was a happy one. Pat worked hard and never missed a day. He'd arrive home after work eager to see his family, and they him. They loved him for his rowdy boisterousness and vivid imagination – he never seemed to run out of new stories to tell the young ones.

For her birthday in 1913, Pat bought Maggie the piano

she had dreamed of owning for years – for 59 pounds, on a payment plan. She'd been taught to play as a girl and missed having music about her, even though Pat and the kids would sing their lungs out at the slightest provocation. Almost every night, after dinner, there would be a concert or a singalong around the piano. When the children were at school and she had some spare time, Maggie would indulge herself with a little classical music.

She could not have foreseen the change in her life that fate had in store.

When the building industry had fallen into a slump after the outbreak of the Great War, Patrick, although now aged fifty-three, was forced to seek other work. He took a job as a fireman and on 26 October 1915, his brigade was called to the Sugar Refinery Wharf at New Farm. A large pile of timber that had been stacked on the wharf for shipment to the northern cane fields had caught fire. It collapsed, crushing Patrick and two other men. The others survived but Pat's injuries were terrible – and fatal.

*

More than four years had passed.

It was a Saturday, mid-morning, in mid-June 1920. Typically, the weather was pleasantly warm, albeit at the onset of winter in Brisbane. The two children sat, a little untidy and barefoot as usual, on the front stoop of the two-bedroom, weatherboard cottage in Stanley Street, where they'd been residing with their mother, Maggie, for the past year or so. It was the most recent in a succession of temporary homes. Maggie had found a way to get them evicted from various addresses in New Farm, Fortitude Valley, Stones Corner and Buranda, usually for not paying the rent. They had no idea how she'd managed to forestall the inevitable at this place, in Woolloongabba. They did know that she'd taken to occasionally bringing men home to drink with her in the kitchen and they stayed late, sometimes until morning.

Harold spoke softly, an air of resignation clearly evident in his voice.

'The cops must've pinched her again, Nellie. I'll go down to the station to see if she's there. If she's not, I'll pick something up for you to eat on me way back.'

He was eleven years old. He and his fourteen-year-old sister hadn't seen Maggie for two days. That didn't concern them very much, really. She always turned up eventually. It had been going on for the past few years. They were used to feeding and fending for themselves when they needed to. When she did finally get home, Harold preferred that it be during the daytime. By then she'd usually had some sleep, was too hung-over to feel maudlin or angry and simply couldn't summon the energy to inflict upon him the habitual, violent attacks that he'd come to dread.

It had been quite a while since he had bothered to make the rounds of Maggie's favourite hangouts to look for her. She'd been permanently barred from most but a few continued to put up with her – she was still somehow able to produce money to push across their bars, after all. Her fits of ill temper, disgusting behaviour and abusive and foul language while under the influence of drink had earned her notoriety. He'd given up chasing after her the night he'd gone into a wine bar in South Brisbane and found her squatting in a corner, urinating on the sawdust-covered floor, much to the amusement of her mostly male drinking partners and to his chilling, cringing embarrassment. He had rarely been successful in coaxing her home before she'd become too drunk. It just wasn't worth trying anymore.

'Please hurry back, Harold. I'm so hungry.'

Nellie's voice was faint. She tried so hard to tough it out but had little of her brother's innate strength. Her dark, straight hair framed a pretty, olive-complexioned face. Her expression gave her a look older than her years. She was of solid, thickset build, unlike her six siblings, who were fairer, tall and slim. 'Be careful, won't you.'

He touched her forearm gently, reassuringly, as he rose. 'Don't worry, Nell. I'll be back as quick as I can,' he said – and in an instant, he was gone.

Although she was older, Nellie deferred willingly to Harold's authority most of the time. He'd taken on board a lot of the responsibility for her care since their father's death. She trusted him implicitly, because he always seemed to know what to do. Nellie knew he had no money whatsoever to buy food. She also knew that if he said he would bring her some, somehow he'd manage to. He despised asking for handouts so she knew he took risks, but she was past caring how he came by it and never questioned his methods. She hated the sickly, light-headed feeling of hunger that she'd had so often these past few years, and they hadn't eaten anything since the previous morning, when Harold had managed to purloin a pair of apples and an orange from a fruit and vegetable store up at Stones Corner. He had developed a brazen and delicate expertise for shoplifting and had been chased by most of the local shop owners.

Shoplifting was pretty easy, he reckoned, provided you were game enough. It was a matter of timing. If you were patient and bided your time until the shopkeeper became busy, it was simple enough to move in and take what you needed. He was quick on his feet and he'd familiarised himself with all of the short cuts, laneways and back streets for miles around, knowledge useful indeed when he needed to make a hasty escape.

He'd even owned a bicycle for a while. He'd 'found' it one day outside a swimming pool up in Spring Hill – could have kept it, too, if he hadn't been unlucky enough for the father of the boy who owned it to recognise the bike as he rode proudly by sometime later. The man reclaimed his son's property and delivered a healthy kick to the young thief's backside, which hurt – a lot. Worse than the pain was the sense of belittlement that accompanied it. Harold decided then and there that this belittlement was something he could live without in the future.

Some kids who spend most of their time playing dangerous games and taking silly risks have the faces to show for it, picking up scars and bruises along the way. Harold did not. He possessed soft, almost feminine features, with pink cheeks, a wide forehead, a kind, full mouth and azure blue eyes. A skinny, square-shouldered boy and tall for his age, he was blessed with the energy of a whirlwind. It catapulted him from his bed early every morning to assail the coming day. His day was normally a frenzy of activity until, usually in the early evening, he'd collapse into bed, hopeful of an uninterrupted night's sleep – something that was not always guaranteed.

He was commandant of the most recklessly energetic and unkempt bunch of larrikins in the poor, working-class inner and south-eastern suburbs of Brisbane. He and his mates engaged in most of the activities enjoyed by little boys, such as playing marbles, football and cricket, and fighting among themselves and teasing girls, when they could be bothered paying any attention to them at all. They loved swimming in summer, although they rarely bothered to pay the entrance fee to any of the City Council's municipal baths, even if they could afford it. They jumped a fence or climbed a wall or a couple of them distracted the gatekeeper by creating a diversion – usually a rowdy 'fight' – while the rest slipped in behind his back. Once inside, they would be lost among the throng of noisy, plunging, playful youngsters who had followed convention and paid their entrance fee.

Above all else, though, the one thing they enjoyed most in summer was cricket, the national game. Proper sporting equipment was in short supply, so they made do with what they could manufacture themselves – often, a fence paling and a rock would do. Sometimes they would manage to 'borrow' something better from the sports kit at East Brisbane State School.

Just as children all over the country did, the boys would spend hours at a time playing Test matches like their cricketing heroes, selecting teams from among themselves to represent Australia and England. 'Borrowing' the equipment was usually Harold's responsibility, so he thought it only fair that he run the show and he always insisted on being captain of Australia. If it happened to rain, they would while away the time indoors, engaged in equally noble pastimes, such as practising dealing and palming playing cards or picking one another's pockets. Harold was a particularly dab hand at pickpocketing and practised hard. He was admired by all among the group for his skill.

Harold was sent to St Joseph's Sisters of Mercy Primary School at Kangaroo Point, as were his brothers and sisters before him – until the nuns declared him uncontrollable. They put it down to the fact that he was without any real parental supervision most of the time. His misconduct and aggression set a bad example to the rest of the children and rather than persevere with him, it was easier to expel him. The state school system was the place for Harold. There he could be among his own kind – children from disadvantaged families, whom the nuns perceived were more inclined to behave poorly. His mother enrolled him at East Brisbane State School. Perhaps they could find a way to deal with him.

His aggressive behaviour caused great anxiety among the teaching staff at his new school as well. They were accustomed to breaking up the occasional altercation in the playground between boys but were at a loss to understand why, unlike most of the other children in their care, this boy preferred to resolve every issue with his fists, favouring disorder over debate. It wasn't simply that he was the kind of boy who boiled over quickly – even at his most aggressive, he always seemed to be in control of his actions. He just seemed to revel in roughhouse behaviour.

As a result, he was embroiled in schoolyard brawls almost daily. Bigger boy or small, no opponent was barred. Harold's delicate facial features lay a trap for any unsuspecting adversary. If they thought they were good fighters, well, he was eager to make manifest their limitations. He had inherited from his Irish ancestors an intense, fiery temper, which simmered permanently close to the surface – but he also had a cool determination to assert himself, which proved too much for his less-qualified opponents to handle. They were mostly tough lads, from tough backgrounds, but toughness wasn't always enough.

Hard though they tried, his teachers couldn't get him to show even the slightest interest in schoolwork. If he didn't feel like going to school, he'd simply take the day off. Truancy became habitual for him and his crew. This, combined with their penchant for mischief, resulted in their becoming well known to the men at the Woolloongabba police station. Most of the cops liked the lads a lot, exchanging cheeky banter back and forth with them. They could see, by the extent of their bumps and bruises, that some of them were being mistreated at home but the kids, Harold especially, had a way of dismissing any inquiries about it, often with humour. The cops hoped that their unsociable, unlawful behaviour would wane with maturity but feared that, for most of them, this wouldn't be the case.

*

Maggie hadn't spent the night in the cells, at least not at Woolloongabba. Harold, with no clue as to her whereabouts, arrived home with a pilfered, already partially eaten loaf of bread, just before Mollie arrived to check on them. Upon learning that they hadn't eaten that day, she sent Nellie to the corner shop for some milk and a little sausage. She could afford no more. She earned one pound, one shilling per week in wages at her new job as a seamstress at Hall's shirt manufacturers. It didn't stretch very far after she paid her rent at Marrs' boarding house in the city, then fed and clothed herself.

Mollie was almost thirty, single and devoutly Catholic. For some years, she'd seriously considered becoming a nun but had decided against it. She was quite beautiful, with long, slightly curly blonde hair – but she was desperately shy and uncomfortable among males, apart from her father, whom she had adored, her priest and her three brothers. Maggie and Patrick's next daughter, Margaret, lived in Charleville, in central Queensland, with her husband, Fred Schoenwald, a subcontractor-carpenter. Mollie had recently returned from spending three years living with them and working as a tailoress at a shop in the town.

When Nellie came back with the food, Mollie made sandwiches and asked her young siblings when they'd last seen their mother.

'Thursday morning,' answered Nellie. 'She said she was going to see someone at the General Hospital about some work but we knew where she was headed, didn't we, Harold?'

Harold nodded his acknowledgment. Maggie always had a convenient excuse to offer the children when she was going out. They'd become much more cynical than was healthy for two youngsters and were rarely fooled, although they invariably hoped for the best: that she'd come home early – and sober.

Since the death of her beloved Patrick, Maggie had fallen into profound depression and alcoholism. Patrick had been the only man she'd ever loved and she had not been able to come to terms with his passing. Spiralling down in all-consuming grief and alcohol abuse, Maggie, who was now fifty-eight, had lost her good looks and friendly, outgoing personality. All trace of her self-respect was gone, to the extent that she thought nothing of occasionally prostituting herself. By some great good fortune, Nellie survived without suffering any form of sexual assault. Harold was not as lucky. He was aroused from his sleep one night to find that he was being fondled by a stranger. His reaction was instant, violent and noisy – the pervert fled the room in pain after receiving a hefty kick to the groin. Pathetically, Maggie drunkenly slept through the entire episode. Harold never bothered to tell her about it. It wasn't worth his trouble – she'd probably only accuse him of making it all up anyway.

They enthusiastically ate most of the sandwiches that Mollie had prepared for them as they sat in the small kitchen at the rear of the house. They didn't finish them off. It didn't take a lot to fill their stomachs these days. Besides, it might be a good idea to save some for later.

Two loud knocks at the front door had a note of foreboding to them. It was the familiar, unmistakable sound of the police calling. Mollie made her way down the narrow hallway. Opening the door, she found Senior Constable James Fraser standing before her.

James was a handsome fellow, tall and broad-shouldered. He removed his cap and placed it under one arm, revealing a mop of thick, blond, unruly hair, which he attempted to straighten when he realised that it was Mollie who'd answered the door. His eyes were blue and his complexion rosy, giving him the look of the Viking. His ancestors, as far back as he knew, were from the southwest of England.

His task, especially as he had been friends with Mollie a long time, was an unpleasant one.

Following procedure, James inquired, in a somewhat official manner, and even though he knew the answer: 'Good morning, Miss. Does Harold William Fingleton reside at this address?'

Falteringly and just as formally, Mollie replied: 'Yes, he does, Constable.'

The sound of their voices reached the kitchen. Harold's and Nellie's eyes locked. Their bodies became tense and they froze.

'Is the boy here at present?'

'Why, yes, he is. What's he been up to this time, James?' Mollie asked, allowing the formality to slide.

James, remaining formal, announced, 'In accordance with this order from the Department of the Minister for State Children, I am to take the youngster in charge and transport him to St Vincent's Orphanage at Nudgee.'

The words barely had passed his lips and Harold was up and running, bolting from the kitchen for the back door. If he could make it to the yard and reach the sanctuary of the lanes and streets he knew so well, he would be able to make a getaway. James had known what to expect, however. Young Fingleton had never gone quietly. No sooner had Harold cleared the back landing than he was collared by two constables who'd been strategically stationed to cover any such escape attempt. He punched and wriggled and kicked out at them as they struggled to hold him in check. They were subjected to a tirade of foul language but they had heard it all from him before. They'd often discussed among themselves their concern as to where he must have learned it all. The answer had become clear to them during their numerous run-ins with Maggie in recent times.

In their experience, they'd found that it was common for a

boy who becomes estranged from his father by his parents' divorce or separation to feel a sense of abandonment. Oddly, even when a father dies – whether as a result of illness, at war or by accident – a bereaved son also often feels that he's been deserted by his father. The police officers saw this manifesting most often in self-resentment and rebellious behaviour. In many cases, the passing of time did nothing to ease such responses. In fact, it only exacerbated them. Harold Fingleton was a typical example. In recent years, his playfully mischievous conduct had developed a more reckless, confrontational edge.

Mollie, who was normally composed and in total control in any given situation, calmed her brother down quickly. He'd always responded to her gentle persuasion. She'd been taken completely by surprise, though, by James's demand. She had known him since their first day at school at St Joseph's Kangaroo Point convent twenty-five years previously. They'd often attended Mass and church socials as a couple during their youth. Mollie had a fair idea that she was never far from James's thoughts, even though they now lived in distant areas of the city and saw each other only occasionally.

'But you know Harold isn't an orphan, James,' she said. 'He lives here with his mother and his sister. There's obviously some mistake.'

'I'm sorry, Mollie, but here's the order,' replied James ruefully, having decided to also dispense with formality. He handed her a notice typewritten on the letterhead of the State Children Department of the Queensland Government. 'Mollie, may I come in? I'd like to have a talk to you about all of this.'

'Yes, of course,' she replied.

The two officers had released their grip on Harold but, just to be sure, James asked them to stand, one each at the front and rear of the house. Then the constable, with Mollie and Harold, walked through the lounge room, which was completely bereft of furniture, to the kitchen. James closed and locked the kitchen window. All of Harold's possible avenues of escape were now sealed.

They all sat around the small square table, Nellie close to Harold. She clasped one of his arms in hers, as if frightened to let go. James spoke first: 'Mollie, are you aware of the cruel treatment that Harold has been receiving for some time now from his mother?'

Mollie hesitated before responding. She looked at her little brother, gently running her hand through his hair, then back at James. 'I know that Harold can be very difficult to control and has to be disciplined often by our mother, James, but apart from that, I don't believe she could treat him badly enough to warrant you people getting involved.'

'I know you've been away in the country for a while, Mollie, but apparently this has been a problem for quite a long time. Looking back, I have to admit I could have made some inquiries myself but it just didn't dawn on me the extent of what was going on,' James said. Casting a glance towards the silent boy, he said: 'Harold, the first time we found you wandering the streets late at night, you told us you'd been out looking for your mum, didn't you? Was that the truth?'

'Yeah,' replied the boy, lying. The truth was that if he was awake when Maggie came in at night and he could manage it, he'd take off and stay away for a while. A few times, he'd spent the night sleeping in a paddock up the road. Most times, he'd return when he was fairly certain that she'd have fallen asleep.

James nodded his acceptance of the lad's statement but wasn't convinced. Turning once again to Mollie, he asked her to read the official notice. It said: 'The Minister has approved that the State boy Harold Fingleton be removed from his mother, Mrs Margaret Fingleton's care and placed in St Vincent's Orphanage, Nudgee.' Enclosed in an official envelope were 'the necessary requisitions for railway tickets and also an authority for admission to the above-mentioned institution'.

'Perhaps this will help you to understand what this is all about,' James said and handed Mollie a handwritten report that he'd removed surreptitiously from his senior sergeant's desk. He glanced again at the boy. Harold was trying to appear calm but his eyes flicked from one adult to the other, bewilderment involuntarily etched on his face.

In the top left-hand corner of the report was a brief notation, signed by the senior sergeant himself: 'House dirty and untidy always – children very intelligent but appear to be half-fed'. The main body of the report outlined how three years previously, Maggie had applied to the department for Harold and Nellie to each be admitted as a 'State Child', citing the death of her husband and her inability to work because of what she described as 'a weak right arm and poor general health'. The 400 pounds that she'd been paid in compensation for Patrick's death and had been held in treasury to be paid in weekly increments had lasted only two years. She confessed to 'not being good at money management' and stated that she now owned no property and had no money in the bank. All but the most basic items of her furniture had been sold to dealers, including her precious piano. Her application was successful, the report noting that 'after due consideration and investigation of her circumstances, monetary assistance, in the amount of eight shillings per child per week, had been granted by the Government Minister'.

The principal expectation of the parent or guardian of a State Child was that they provide food, shelter and care. The child was regarded as 'boarded out to the parent and subject to rigid inspection'. Any failure to satisfy the stated requirements or 'misbehaviour in the home', such as drunkenness or cruelty on the part of the parent or guardian, would not be tolerated and the child 'may be removed'. State Children were 'liable to be boarded out, adopted or apprenticed to trade anywhere in the State without reference to parents or relatives and without informing them what has been done'. When State Children reached the age of fourteen, they were 'discharged' and benefits ceased. This had been the case with Nellie the previous August.

'May I say something, please, Constable?' Nellie asked.

'Yes, of course you can, Nellie,' replied James.

Nellie turned sad, dewy eyes towards Mollie. 'Mollie, I know I wrote to you and Margaret and told you Mum was being cruel to Harold. I should have told you more but I didn't want to worry you too much. The truth is that she's taken to using a plank of three-by-two to hit him with. It makes me cry sometimes when I see some of the awful bruises on his body and legs. As much as I try, I can't stop her. She seems to become really strong when she's mad.

'A couple of weeks ago, she was belting him so hard and Harold was screaming so loudly that two men came in from the street. They said they thought someone was being murdered. Then last week, she pulled him out of bed at nine o'clock for no reason and put him in the shower naked and turned on the cold water and started to belt him with a leather belt. She was screaming that she'd murder him. That time the lady from next door came in and took Harold home with her and looked after him until the next morning.

'I don't understand why she attacks Harold all the time. She never, ever hits me. She works herself up into such a state. I've seen her throw herself on the floor and scream hysterically for ages. Every now and then, Kitty comes around and tries to settle Mum down.' Kitty, who was about to turn twenty, had been married to Michael Dixon, a railway worker from Buranda, for nearly two years. Planning to have a large family, they'd already had a son, whom they named John Joseph, and Kitty was pregnant again. 'Sometimes she stays for a couple of days and everything's peaceful but she has so much to do to look after her own family. When she goes, Mum runs straight out and starts drinking again and it all starts all over again. Harold and I hate it when Kitty leaves.' The longer Nellie spoke, the more her tears flowed and her voice gradually dwindled to a melancholy whisper.

'All of that is in this report,' James told Mollie. 'The people who were responsible enough to intervene came over to the station to fill out complaints against your mother, then we sent reports to the State Minister's office.'

Mollie's shoulders slumped and tears welled in her eyes. A frown spread across her brow as she slowly shook her head and stammered, 'I – I had no idea it had come to this.' Harold said nothing. Mollie reached out and clasped his and Nellie's hands, which were now clenched together on the table. 'I'm so, so sorry, children . . . I should have done something.'

James broke in: 'You couldn't be expected to do anything if you didn't know what was really going on, Mollie.'

Harold continued to offer nothing to the discussion. His mother was always so full of remorse after her attacks and

Harold always forgave her – not grudgingly but with the generosity only a child can muster for the parent he adores. He fancied that he understood her state of mind. Like their mother, the children all missed their father terribly. For Harold, their time together had been all too brief. His memory of his father was now a fading, spectral outline. What remained were only unanswered questions as to why he had gone away at all. Over time they would develop into obscure, unexpressed feelings of forlornness that would continue to haunt him throughout his life.

The room had fallen silent. Mollie and Nellie struggled to come to terms with the gravity of the situation, each full of concern for her brother, each grimly aware that now the official decision had been made, it would have to be enforced. Harold sat still, quietly confident yet that their eldest sister could come up with a solution the policeman might agree to that would allow him to remain at home. Mollie was an adult and once you became an adult, you could do anything, he reckoned.

There was no rescue plan forthcoming, however. Mollie was left with no choice but to allow James to take her little brother with him. She washed Harold's face and hands and helped him dress in a shirt, breeches, knee-length socks and black, scuffed shoes. A small neat cap completed the outfit.

Mollie tenderly attempted to reassure him: 'I don't fully understand how they can do this, darling but I promise you

I'll do everything I can to get you home again as soon as possible, so try not to worry. The Sisters of Mercy run the orphanage and you'll find that they'll be kind to you. Promise me you'll be a good boy and do what you're told, won't you.'

Harold nodded but was far from convinced about most of this. The couple of years he'd spent at the convent school with the Sisters of Mercy had taught him that they were not always so kind and gentle, especially with naughty boys. He hoped that Mollie would be able to keep her word but he was more bothered by the fact that it had come to this. It must all be his fault – he was a bad kid and this was just what he deserved. He didn't know what was coming next and for once an uncommon feeling swept through him: he felt scared, really scared, and even though he tried not to show it, James could see it in his usually defiant eyes. He saw in the boy a frightened child he hadn't seen before.

Mollie prepared another sandwich for the train journey, politely offering one to each of the policemen, which, equally politely, they declined. She held her distraught sister close to her as Harold was escorted to the police station. She was shocked as she became aware, from a distance, of how frail and thin his body looked. They watched from the front landing as the group passed around the corner onto Main Street and out of sight.

2
Off to St Vincent's

*The coach jumbled us insensibly
into some kind of familiarity*

Sir Richard Steele (1672–1729)

Before Constable Fraser could deliver Harold to his destination, he had to first complete some of the limitless paperwork that the government required. It was a duty made even more tedious by the knowledge that the information he clattered onto the forms via the old station typewriter could very well finish up forgotten in a file somewhere, possibly never again to be viewed by human eyes. It wasn't made any easier by the constant, repetitious nagging of one H.W. Fingleton, who, instead of sitting quietly as he was asked to, constantly reminded the young cop just how long all of this was taking.

When finally the documentation had been completed, the early afternoon had slipped by. James bid his workmates goodbye for the day. By the time he had seen young Fingleton to the orphanage, his shift would be finished and he would go home to nearby Northgate, where he lived with his parents.

The train bound for Nudgee left at four o'clock from Central station, which was a brisk fifty-minute walk from the Gabba through South Brisbane and the centre of the city. James walked with one arm around the lad's shoulder. What might have appeared to be a gesture of affection was actually a precaution against Harold making a bolt for freedom. At Central they boarded a steam train and set off on the hour-long ride northeast to Banyo station.

Harold was scarcely able to conceal his excitement. This was his first train ride and he temporarily put aside his dread at the uncertainty of what was to come. He couldn't resist the urge to stand with his head out of the open window, ignoring James's exhortations to be careful. It didn't take long for him to find out that if you stood with your head out of the window of a Puffing Billy, you got your mouth and eyes filled with thick black smoke that contained minuscule particles of burnt coal. It tasted awful and stung his eyes but he found that if he squinted hard and closed his mouth, it only finished up in his nose. Every now and then he would take a break, sit down and get some relatively fresh air but before long would be back at it again. The policeman was thrilled to see the essence of the little boy return. He was filled with remorse for the kid's plight. He knew that Harold had witnessed more and suffered much more damage already in his brief life than any child should.

Eventually, the novelty wore off and Harold returned to his seat next to James. He opened the paper bag containing the sandwich that Mollie had prepared for him but couldn't raise the appetite to eat it. He offered it to James. 'Do you want this?'

James shook his head. 'No thanks, Harold.'

Harold disposed of it through the open window.

James shook his head, feigning despair.

The journey would soon end and Harold appeared to grow thoughtful. He wasn't the first child James had delivered into the hands of the Sisters of Mercy. James felt some added responsibility for this boy, though, mainly because of his fondness for Mollie. He also could not deny that he harboured a genuine affection for the kid, which Harold had long sensed and was comfortable with. James decided to offer him some advice. 'You know, Harold, if you behave yourself and do as you're told, life will be easy enough for you out here,' he said. 'You'll be among a lot of other kids in the same boat as you. If you put your mind to it, you'll get along with them all okay. The nuns are good women and if you don't give them any trouble, they won't give you any. But they have a big job on their hands looking after so many children and it isn't easy for them. You'll learn soon enough that they can run out of patience sometimes if you step out of line. So be good and you'll get through it no trouble. Mollie will do whatever she can to get you back home again, you know that. Let's hope we see one another again sooner rather than later.'

Harold just nodded and looked straight ahead. He wasn't so worried about any harsh treatment he might receive. He could handle anything physical that they could dish out, he reckoned. But he would miss Nellie and his mates – and his mother, despite all her faults. 'Will you help Mollie to get me back home if you can?'

'You can rest assured that if there's anything I can do, I will. I'll even try to come and visit you every now and then if you like.'

'Thanks, Jim.' As he said it, he turned to his travelling companion with a cheeky glint in his eye and a half-grin on his face.

The cop involuntarily chuckled and grinned back. No one ever called him Jim and Harold knew it. And besides, he was supposed to address him as 'Constable'. For James, it was charmingly typical of the lad. It was what set him apart from the other youngsters. He was habitually mischievous and it appealed to James's sense of humour greatly.

From Banyo station they walked two miles or so up a hill,

along an unpaved road, to St Vincent's. They chatted animatedly all of the way, James again walking with his arm around Harold's shoulder. This time, it was an expression not of precaution but of warmth and fondness. They arrived at the unassuming steel gate of the orphanage in remarkably good humour, considering the task at hand, and entered. The gate was sprung and closed of its own accord with a rusty screech and a clang behind them. The sound chilled Harold and caused some of his stress to return. They proceeded down a lengthy gravel path to arrive at the entrance to a very large, two-storeyed white building. It was stately, with wide verandahs on the front and sides on both levels.

James gave an authoritative knock on the door, then removed his policeman's cap as it was opened by a huge woman clothed in a black habit. She was by far the biggest woman Harold had ever seen and her bulk seemed to fill the entire doorway. Her bright red face looked ready to burst from the constraints of the starched white coif that covered her forehead and ears and wrapped severely under her chin. She wore a knee-length black veil. A white guimpe, also heavily starched, covered her broad shoulders and massive chest. A leather cincture and an oversized set of rosary beads surrounded her ample waistline and a pair of black thin-soled boots completed the rather austere habit of the Sisters of Mercy. Apart from her face, the only parts of her body visible were her hands, which were proportionately large. The woman's appearance unnerved the boy momentarily.

James was trained from as far back as his Catholic school days to show respect to everyone – in a position of authority or otherwise – but the good humour that had developed during their trip still remained and something about the situation and the sight of the woman was irresistibly amusing. Unfortunately, his and Harold's glances met and they let out very audible guffaws, followed by a brace of self-conscious giggles. The pair quickly gathered themselves together, striving desperately not to bubble over again.

The nun sensed the cause of their outburst of jollity and expressed her disapproval with a resounding 'Hmmph'. Then she snorted, 'Yes, Constable, whom do we have here?' Her voice rumbled across the rapidly gathering twilight like a foghorn and reverberated down the hallway behind her.

'His name is Harold Fingleton, Sister. He is eleven years old. Here are his case particulars.'

'Thank you, Constable.' She snatched the folder from James with one hand, grabbed Harold roughly by the shoulder with the other and unceremoniously yanked him through the doorway. As she did so, the policeman and the lad attempted to say goodbye but the door slammed in James's face, leaving him standing with one hand raised out in front of him but nobody to bid farewell to. He donned his cap, slowly turned on his heel and made his way from the orphanage.

3
Welcome!

A hard beginning maketh a good ending

John Heywood (1497–c.1580), *Proverbs*

'Stand there and be still.'

Harold stood there and was still.

The large nun roughly removed his cap and thrust it into his hands. She turned and addressed her superior, at the same time handing her the folder James had given her. 'Mother, this is the latest arrival. He seems to be a boy with quite a sense of humour.'

'Thank you, Sister.' The more senior nun was exactly the opposite of the other in appearance, voice and manner. She sat at an expansive, solid-looking desk in a large office befitting her station as head of the orphanage and Mother Superior to the nuns. Hung upon the walls were the obligatory pictures of the Sacred Heart, the then Pope,

Benedict XV, and Our Blessed Lady, the Virgin Mary, dressed in pale blue and white, standing on a cloud, her eyes turned towards the heavens. In one corner, on a pedestal, stood a statue of the bearded Saint Vincent, patron saint of the poor. Harold had noticed a similar one, only larger, in the courtyard he had been led through moments before.

She perused the information contained in the folder, then looked up at him. 'Well, he looks reasonably clean, anyway. Have you checked his head and ears, Sister?'

'I haven't as yet, Mother.'

'Well, would you do so please and see to his ablutions.'

'Of course, Mother.'

'Very well. Thank you, Sister. That will be all.'

Harold was horrified. *Ablutions! What the bloody hell are ablutions? And how the bloody hell is she gonna see to 'em?* he thought. He'd never heard of ablutions. It sounded awfully like it might be some kind of medicine. He hated medicine.

The nun grabbed him by the scruff with one hand and half-dragged, half-carried him from the office and through a doorway that led outside. They proceeded along a tin-roofed wooden landing with trellised, vine-covered windbreaks on either side. Harold was impressed with the woman's strength but if she didn't loosen her grip on his throat soon, he reckoned, he'd choke to death. 'We don't enjoy boys with senses of humour here,' she said threateningly. 'We'd just as soon they simply show respect and behave themselves.' The nun was holding him like a bag of apples. His legs were swinging wildly. He endeavoured to gain some control but his feet were barely touching the ground when they arrived at an outbuilding, which he discovered to be the bathing block. Once inside, in a dimly lit room, he was deposited in a corner and instructed, once again, to 'stand there and be still'. Once again, he complied.

He was confronted with the spectacle of some forty or fifty naked boys – all, he guessed, about his own age or a little older. They were mostly skinny and frail looking and their complexions were all quite pallid. Some stood with their arms folded around themselves and their shoulders hunched in an effort to stay warm.

They were standing in separate lines, waiting to take their turn in one of four bathtubs in a row. Another thirty or so had already finished their baths and were drying themselves.

'Disrobe and stand in line,' the nun told Harold.

He did so. As he waited his turn, he noticed that the bath water was not being emptied and replenished. One grubby little boy after another took his turn in the water, which was taking on a hue that was difficult to describe. It was a kind of brownish, yellowy green.

By the time his turn came around, he'd become extremely disinclined to immerse himself in a chilly pool of filthy water. Standing by the side of one of the baths, bravely, but ill-advisedly, he piped up, 'Can you change the water?'

Harold's request had the same effect as the crack of a stockwhip ringing through the room. The boys' hushed chatter ceased; in the silence, a pin dropping would have sounded like an exploding firecracker. Some of the older boys glanced at each other and winced, knowingly. Harold heard a couple of them mutter, almost in unison, 'Oh no.'

Harold's new-found nemesis came charging in his direction. With a heavy right hand, she slapped him almost senseless, making his ears ring loudly. 'Get in!' she roared. He obliged. There was no soap but he wasn't going to risk asking for any, so he gritted his teeth and pretended to wash himself with the putrid water. Having finished, he semi-dried off with one of the very damp and smelly towels he found on the floor and then dressed. Until now he'd never had a bath that made him feel dirtier afterwards than before he got in it. He noticed that the other boys had lined up in pairs, so he figured that he should join one of the queues and follow whoever was in front of him. His ears continued to make a ringing noise. It sounded as if his head was full of cicadas.

He had learned his first lessons in institutional life and he made a couple of mental notes – rules to memorise and follow.

Rule one: Never, ever get caught at the end of a queue.

Rule two: Go quietly whenever possible.

He was about to follow the line wherever it might lead him when he was again confronted by his assailant.

'Just a moment, you,' she said. He froze on the spot where he stood. 'Come with me.'

Shit, he thought, *here come the bloody ablutions.*

He accompanied the nun along another landing, which led to an adjacent building identical in shape and size to the one that they'd just left. This one turned out to be the toilet block. It contained about twenty cubicles, without doors, along one side. Each cubicle housed a wooden bench with a hole in it and a five-gallon steel drum beneath the hole. A box of torn-up strips of newspaper and some sawdust sat to one side of the cubicle. These were the lavatories.

Along the other side of the building was another bench; this one was taller, some thirty inches above the floor. Circular holes about ten inches in diameter had been cut into it, spaced a couple of feet apart. In each hole rested an enamel-coated steel basin, with a tap above it. On the floor in front of the bench there was a three-inch-high slatted timber platform, through which water would drain to the concrete floor below.

'Stand there and —'

'Yeah, I know, be still.'

He had no idea what prompted him to finish her sentence for her but he wished he hadn't, because it earned him yet another crashing clout to the head. He spent the next few moments gathering his wits while the nun half-filled one of the basins with cold water. He watched through myriad, quite pretty, swirling stars while she donned a pair of thick rubber gloves. It did occur to him to inquire as to why she might need gloves but this time he remembered rule two. He was busy congratulating himself for his good sense as she wet his hair with water from the basin and removed the cap from a bottle of odd-smelling liquid. She squeezed some out and proceeded to massage it into his scalp. It tingled at first and then began to burn. She continued to rub his scalp and it continued to burn, until it burned so much that he could stand it no longer.

'Whaddya think you're bloody doing?' he screamed and pushed her away with both hands, causing her to topple over backwards. He was concentrating so heavily on trying to soothe his scalp with cold running water that it took a moment for him to register that as she fell, her head hit the wall quite violently. She lay there, badly dazed.

In the confusion, the entire contents of the basin had spilt, drenching his clothes and most of the wooden platform for a few feet around where he stood. He succeeded in rinsing some of the solution from his hair but his scalp still burned. A quantity of the evil concoction had found its way into one eye and as he was feverishly attempting to wash it out, he failed to notice that the nun had struggled to her feet. He

Welcome!

caught sight of the huge right fist a moment too late and received the full brunt of the woman's power, falling to the ground. Her effort caused her to slip on the wet platform. Time momentarily stalled and as Harold lapsed into unconsciousness, he heard her let out an involuntary, very shrill kind of 'Whoops!' She, too, fell, her head smashing onto the concrete floor with a fearful crunch.

When he awakened, he was lying in a rather uncomfortable bed, he knew not where exactly. He peered around the room, which was dark but for the moonlight that entered through double windows close to the ceiling all around the perimeter. The shafts of moonlight created images on the wall opposite where he lay that resembled sets of eerie eyes staring threateningly down upon him. His scalp felt irritated, which brought to mind the events of the evening. He touched his head to see if he still had any hair. He was sure he wouldn't, that it all would have been burnt off, and was relieved to find that it was still where it should be. The eye that had been invaded by the awful mixture was very watery. He blinked uncontrollably and his vision in that eye was blurred. He pushed himself up on one elbow. As his unaffected eye became more accustomed to the darkness, he decided that he must have been taken to hospital. The room was much the same as the ward at the Royal Brisbane where he'd spent a few nights to have his tonsils removed when he was seven years old. Beds containing still, small forms lined each wall of the room and there was a row of yet more beds in the middle. He reasoned that there must be a lot of sick children around. A few of them were whimpering for their mothers, just as they had at the Royal.

The day had been all too eventful and tiring, so he was happy to fall back to sleep. The last thing he was aware of thinking was: *Well, at least they forgot to gimme the bloody ablutions.*

4
Bloody Mass

Light half-believers of our casual creeds

Matthew Arnold (1822–88)

All too soon for Harold, it was Sunday morning.

The children were startled to consciousness at five o'clock sharp by the altogether unnecessarily loud clanging of a bell rung at the main doorway by one of the nuns. He realised immediately that he was not in hospital after all. They didn't ring bells in hospitals, as far as he knew. As he came to his senses, he felt extreme pain in the left side of his jaw.

The room reeked with the smell of damp urine. He discovered that he had somehow been changed into a full-length cotton nightshirt. It bothered him that he was naked beneath it. He saw that he'd spent the night in a bunk next to a doorway that led to a verandah.

'What's your name?' Harold asked the boy in the bunk closest to his.

The boy answered in a whisper, 'Tommy – what's yours?'

'Harold.' His voice echoed around the dormitory. He hadn't really noticed until now how quiet the place was. Suddenly he had the attention of every boy in the room.

Tommy placed an admonishing right index finger to his lips. 'Shoosh!'

Harold looked about him, wondering what the problem was.

'We aren't s'posed to talk in here,' Tommy, still whispering, advised him.

They were lucky this time. The nun in charge of the dorm had temporarily stepped outside.

'Fair dinkum?'

'Yeah.'

For the time being at least, Harold decided it might be wise to watch what Tommy did and follow suit.

First, they were to make their bunks tidy. That was easy enough. Just straighten out a sheet and fold it under the edges of what passed for a mattress at St Vincent's – simple straw stuffed into a canvas covering. They called this type of mattress a palliasse, he would learn. It had leather loops sewn to the corners, which were used to attach it to a slatted wooden bed frame. There were no pillows.

He followed Tommy's lead and changed into his clothes,

which he found hanging on a wooden peg beside his bunk. He noticed that there was a numbered metal tag screwed to the bed frame. His number was 78. Tommy, number 77, folded his nightshirt and placed it neatly at the foot of his bed. Harold did the same, although not quite as neatly.

Tommy was smaller than Harold, plain-looking and pale, with straight, blond hair and shoulders that were slightly round, giving him the look of someone older who had the weight of the world to carry. Again he spoke in a whisper: 'Did you wet the bed?'

'Of course not!' Harold replied in his most offended tone.

Tommy fired back with another resounding 'Shoosh!'

Harold couldn't remember ever having wet his bed. He was insulted at the suggestion that he might have and raised himself up to his full height, ready to give this kid a lesson in manners.

Tommy remained absolutely calm, unconcerned and unimpressed by the new fellow's threatening posture. 'Keep your shirt on – those kids have.' He nodded in the direction of a number of lads who were carrying their drenched bedding from the dorm to the verandah.

'Whadda they doing?' Harold asked, now in a much quieter voice – maintaining control of his shirt, as advised.

'When anyone wets the mattress, they have to take it outside and hang it over the railing to dry in the sun.'

'What if it's raining?'

'That's their bad luck. They sleep on a wet bed. Plus they get a belting from Sister Mary Francis as well.'

'Who's Sister Mary Francis?'

Tommy sighed. Was this kid ever going to stop asking questions? 'She sleeps over there in the corner. She's called the dorm mistress.'

Harold looked in the direction Tommy had nodded towards. He saw a small enclosure that he hadn't noticed before. It was open topped, about eight feet square, with walls about the same height. The door was ajar.

'They reckon there's one in every dorm. The nuns call 'em cells. Buggered if I know why.'

'Whadda we do now?' said Harold.

'We line up and go to the lavatory and then wash our face and hands. While you're there, try to sneak a mouthful of water if you can.'

'Why?'

''Cause you'll be thirsty all day if you don't. After breakfast, we hardly ever get anything to drink. We're always thirsty – but they don't care.'

Then they all lined up in pairs and marched towards the toilet block.

Harold had already forgotten rule one. He found himself washing his face in a bowl of dirty water. No chance of a drink this time. Again there was no soap. He gave himself a stern reminder about the queue thing.

They marched back to the dormitory.

'Do we get any breakfast?'

'After Mass.'

'Bloody Mass. I knew that'd be on.'

While they'd been washing, a set of 'good' clothes had been placed upon each bunk. There were a white short-sleeved cotton shirt, grey serge calf-length shorts with a leather belt, knee-length grey woollen socks and black leather shoes. They each busily changed into them. In a few minutes, they were transformed into a very angelic-looking group, ready for Sunday Mass at five-thirty a.m.

Harold was pleasantly surprised to find that his outfit fitted him rather well. He was not at all keen on the idea of Mass, though. He'd only ever attended when Mollie and Kitty had been at home, and only to keep them happy. He couldn't understand anything the priest was saying, apart from the sermon. That was always too long and boring and never made much sense, either. What little he did understand indicated clearly that he was well and truly on his way to hell anyway. He'd promised himself that one day he'd find out what the sins of fornication and adultery were and how one went about committing them. They seemed to be a pet topic of the priest at St Stephen's Cathedral in the city, where Mollie and Kitty liked to go each Sunday.

The convent chapel was a beautiful mini-cathedral filled with all of the normal trappings. There were vases of fresh flowers at the feet of numerous statues of the Saviour, His mother and some of the saints. The Stations of the Cross were depicted upon the walls and stained-glass windows portrayed dramatic, colourful religious images. It could hold about one hundred worshippers.

Sunday Mass, apart from mealtimes, was the only time that the 'big' boys and girls ever came within remote proximity of one another. The girls sat on one side of the aisle, the boys on the other. A nun was seated at the aisle end of every fifth pew to ensure that there was no contact of any kind between any of them. The children were required to look to the front at all times. Suitable punishment awaited anyone sinful enough not to do so. The girls, too, were dressed in their Sunday best. Each wore a long-sleeved, ankle-length white frock and a veil, which was also, of course, white.

Harold took Holy Communion when it was his turn, even though he hadn't been to Confession for the longest time. To not take Communion, he figured, was only asking for trouble. The gluey wafer thing that the priest placed on his tongue clung to the roof of his mouth and he knew it would remain there unless he scraped it off with his finger. This was forbidden: one must not defile the Body of Christ in such a way. He found it impossible to remove it with his tongue, as did most of the others. They were making strange faces in their endeavours to do so. It was still on the roof of Harold's mouth as they all filed into the dining room for breakfast. Finally, deciding to risk eternal damnation, he detached it with his forefinger and at last it was gone.

Harold wondered what might be on the menu. He could smell food cooking and it smelt delicious. Could it be bacon and sausages? Maybe they were getting eggs and tomato and buttery toast? The aroma was making him salivate. Agog with anticipation, he took his place at the breakfast table next to Tommy.

He was right. There were sausages and bacon, eggs and tomato and toast – but not for the children. They were for the Mother Superior and her inferiors, who sat at a table at the head of the hall. The children sat at three long rows of tables. The boys were at the back of the room, separated from the girls at the front by the dorm mistresses, most of them still novices.

The bill of fare for the children was less appetising by far. Each received a large glass of water and one well-cooked sausage served with something watery and green. Harold hoped it might be a vegetable of some kind. He was rather relieved to find that it was at least completely tasteless, whatever it was. He lodged a complaint with Tommy about the food but learned in short order that conversation at the meal table was not tolerated, either. A patrolling nun taught him this lesson with a clout behind the right ear and a

'Quiet!' He was thankful that she didn't hit him on the other side. His jaw still ached and it was difficult to chew. Then he received what was to pass for tea, in a chipped enamel mug. The tea had an odd taste, Harold thought. He wasn't sure if it was the tea itself or the mug. Detecting an unpalatable metallic tang, he decided that it was probably the latter.

Sunday breakfast was over but before they were dismissed, one of the nuns announced the names of three boys. Harold's was among them. They were to proceed immediately to the Mother Superior's office.

This time Harold made sure he was first in line. It gained him nothing, except first go at any potential punishment. It was just good practice at rule one. The other two boys offered no resistance.

He was ordered to stand before the Mother Superior's desk, facing her and another, very old nun, who sat, slightly slumped, eyes downcast, in a chair to the Mother Superior's left. He wasn't entirely sure that she was even alive, so still and quiet was she, until he noticed her right forefinger and thumb moving ever so slowly along her set of rosary beads and the barely discernible movement of her lips.

The Mother Superior asked him to recount his version of the events that had taken place the previous evening. He pleaded amnesia, figuring that it was his most reliable defence. He certainly wasn't going to offer any information that he didn't have to. When he complained to the Mother

Superior about his aching jaw, she ignored him and again questioned him about what happened. But he'd been grilled before by the police at the Gabba station. They could have told the nun that he wouldn't crack. She didn't tell him that Sister Mary Teresita had been removed to the Mater Misericordiae Hospital in a coma after they'd both been found in the toilet block and that an X-ray had revealed that she'd suffered a fractured skull. He complained again about his sore jaw and again he was ignored.

Finally, he was told to wait outside the office. Minutes later he was recalled.

Mother Mary spoke. 'Harold, for the time being, you may consider yourself very fortunate. Until we speak to Sister Mary Teresita and get her version of events, we have no idea of what actually transpired last night. There are no direct witnesses. If we discover that you have been responsible for her injury, you will be sent to the state reformatory for boys. In the meantime you will be expected to be obedient and behave yourself.'

He was dismissed with instructions to return to his dorm and change into his day clothes. Once he'd done this, his dorm mistress accompanied him to the first-floor balcony, where he joined a group of nine other boys whose task it was to sweep, scrub and polish the timber floor. The system was that two of them swept, then a row of four, each supplied with a hand brush, scrubbed the floor with soapy water. The last group mopped up the soapy mess. After it was given time to dry, they all returned, half to apply polish, the rest to buff it by hand with rags. Another group did the same to the floors inside. Every child above the age of five took their turn at this job, on a roster system.

This accomplished, there was time for some religious doctrine. The children would study various aspects of their religion, from basic catechism to more fundamental dogma, depending upon their age. This concluded at midday, when they gathered in the dining room for lunch. Another tasteless repast awaited them. It amounted to a chunk of plain bread, torn from the loaf, followed by a cup of St Vincent's very finest metallic tea. That consumed, they were released into the playground for what Harold would learn was their only free time of the week. This was their chance to be as noisy and carefree as they liked. Most took full advantage, while some chose to sit quietly alone or in small cliques.

Ever the competitor, Harold challenged Tommy to a race to a large tree at the top of the playground. Tommy, who was less active than most kids but was prepared to participate nonetheless, was soundly, disgracefully beaten.

When he arrived at the bench at the foot of the tree, they sat together and talked. Tommy was not like any of the boys in Harold's gang but Harold liked him. This boy was much quieter and there was a solid quality in him. Harold sensed that he'd be someone he could trust.

Bloody Mass

Inevitably, Harold asked, 'How long have you been here?' Tommy told Harold that he was nearly eleven, as far as he knew. He wasn't sure of his birth date. He came from Sandgate, a suburb close to Nudgee. His parents had abandoned him and he'd been delivered to this place late one night about a year before by a police sergeant.

A large group of lads, about forty Harold reckoned, had started to play cricket. In another section of the playground, a lesser number of boys were kicking a football back and forth. It was football season and he thought for a moment that he might go over and teach them all how to kick a ball. He reconsidered. He'd been watching the cricketers and liked what he saw. None of these blokes could bat or bowl to save themselves. They'd never get him out.

'Do you wanna have a hit with these blokes, Tommy?'

'Nah, I'll be right here.'

'Righto.'

The usual rules of back-yard cricket applied. If you bowled the batsman out, you were next man in to bat.

He approached the big red-haired, freckle-faced, gangly kid who'd been doing most of the bowling and giving most of the orders. It was clear that he was boss of the yard.

'Give's a bowl, will you, mate.'

The redhead eyed him disdainfully. 'Yeah, next week,' came his reply. Shoving Harold heavily in the chest with one hand, he readied himself to run in and continue his over.

No Australian captain had ever experienced such rudeness.

Moments – and a few heated words later – it was on.

Nothing entertained and excited the boys more than a good fight, nor generated such a din. Kids charged over to watch the fracas from all directions. The crowd roared.

Before he had a chance to beat the big kid to a pulp, along with a smaller pest of a boy who'd been attacking him from his left flank, the racket attracted the attention of the playground mistresses. He was on his way back to Mother Mary Brigid's office before he could say 'Howzat!'

5
Crime and Punishment

Crimes, like virtues are their own rewards

George Farquhar (1678–1707)

The four boys were hustled, breathless, into the convent building by Sister Aloysius. The newly polished floors made a squeaking sound under their bare feet. They were told to sit on two wooden benches on opposite sides of the hallway outside the office. They were under strict instructions to observe absolute silence while Sister Aloysius consulted with her superior. Mother Brigid would deal with them in good time.

The redhead and his mate sat on one bench and Harold and Tommy on the other.

'Tommy?' Harold said. In all of the confusion, he hadn't noticed him until now. 'Whaddya doing here, Tom?' Harold spoke in as quiet a voice as he could manage, from one side of his mouth.

Tommy replied, also whispering, 'I saw there was two on one, so I tried to help you.'

Harold was deeply impressed. 'Jeez, thanks, mate. I woulda been all right, but thanks anyway. Can you fight?'

Tommy shrugged his shoulders. 'I dunno. Don't think so.'

They both began to laugh and the boys sitting opposite, in chorus, shooshed them.

'Ah shuddup,' Harold fired back – too loudly, as it turned out, because Sister Aloysius had just opened the office door to come and fetch them at that moment. He received yet another cuff across the back of his head for his disobedience.

'You were told to be quiet!' she reminded him.

The nun entered the office once again and exited seconds later, returning to her playground duties.

'Shit, they don't mind hitting you round here, do they?' Harold observed, to no one in particular.

Tommy didn't have anything to say. He'd kept a low profile at St Vincent's. He was naturally even-tempered and kept out of trouble. What he'd done on this occasion was totally out of character. To Harold, it was evidence that Tom was someone he'd like to have for a mate. He knew there weren't many who would've done what Tom had, even among his tough mates in East Brisbane, who had known him for much, much longer. The friendship and absolute trust in each other the boys established in that moment was to endure for the rest of their lives.

The four lads were summoned into the office and stood in line facing the Mother Superior.

Mother Brigid addressed Harold first, stating the obvious: 'This is the second time you have visited this office for creating havoc and you haven't even been here one full day yet.'

Harold shrugged.

'Don't you have anything to say for yourself?'

'Nuh.'

'That will be "No, Mother", if you don't mind.'

'But you're not me mother!'

'That does not matter. You shall address me as Mother always and you shall not talk back to me or any of the nuns, who are here to look after you. And you shall address them each as Sister and show them respect at all times. You already may be in serious trouble. You will find that we do not tolerate repeated bad behaviour here. If you do not learn to behave yourself, your time with us will be short and very unpleasant for you. Do you understand?'

Harold nodded.

'Have you lost your voice? Do you understand?'

'Yeah.'

'Yes, Mother!' She was beginning to demonstrate some of her own Irish heritage.

Harold sighed dramatically, but for once, conformed. 'Yes, Mother.'

She widened her gaze from him ever so slowly and addressed them as a group. 'Now, the rest of you have been at this place for some time. You should all be aware of the rules about fighting. It is strictly forbidden at all times, for any reason and under any circumstances. Isn't that correct?'

The redhead blurted, 'But I didn't start it, Mother, he did,' pointing a finger directly at Harold.

'Yeah, Mother, he did,' echoed his smaller accomplice.

Harold was less than impressed by their lack of courage under fire.

She turned her attention back to him. 'Is this true?'

'Could be.'

'Could be, Mother!' Her cheeks had begun to redden.

He sighed again, casting his eyes towards the ceiling in frustration. 'Could be, Mother.'

'What do you mean, "Could be"? Either it is or it isn't.'

Harold said nothing in response, just shrugged his shoulders.

'What about you, Master Thomas? I am not used to seeing you in here and I am disappointed in you. Whom do you say started the fight?'

Tom's response again impressed his new mate. 'What fight, Mother?'

'You know very well what fight!'

'I dunno, Mother,' Tom replied with a shrug. At least he knew the rules about addressing the nuns.

'I see.'

Mother Brigid had seen more than the boys could have realised. Born in Ireland, as a child she had been sold by her parents to the Church to be trained as a nun – a not uncommon practice in that day. As a teenager she had been sent to Australia to join the Sisters of Mercy in 1877, only sixteen years after the order had come to Brisbane to set up its first home for orphan children in rented cottages at New Farm.

She and her family had lived through troubled times and knew the meaning of tragedy and loss, so she recognised and admired solidarity when she saw it. She'd seen it in Harold and Tommy but could not condone it in this case. The boys must learn.

The redhead again piped up. 'He did start it, Mother, honest he did.'

'Yeah, Mother, honest he did,' echoed his sidekick.

She ignored their accusations. By now she was beyond caring who started what. She stood, removed a heavily stitched leather strap from a drawer and walked around to the front of the desk. Rolling up her right sleeve, she said,

'Well, you each shall be punished in any case. Turn around and drop your trousers, please.'

The small one began to whimper.

'Stop that, or you shall receive extra,' she told him.

He ceased whimpering, but was terrified and lost control of his bladder, wetting the office floor with urine.

'You disgusting boy,' she cried and, grabbing him by his shoulder, delivered six hard whacks to his bare bottom, which only made him leak even more. He leapt and twisted to try to evade the strap, and the other three dodged and dived to avoid being hit by the spray of urine. Harold and Tommy laughed out loud, enjoying the fun. The redhead remained sombre throughout. When the first thrashing was finished, Mother Superior said, 'Now you shall go to the kitchen and see Sister Mary Alphonse. Tell her what you have done and ask her to give you a mop and some hot, soapy water in a bucket. Then bring it all back here and clean up this mess.'

Sobbing loudly, the boy left the room.

The redhead was next. He began to plead unashamedly. 'Please, please, Mother, don't hit me, please. I won't do it again, I promise.'

She had less sympathy for him, in particular, than he could have imagined.

'Bend over,' she roared.

He reacted to each cut of the strap with a shrill 'Ow', weeping and crying out more loudly with each one.

Harold nudged Tommy knowingly. 'I knew this bloke would have no guts,' he whispered.

Mother Mary Brigid pretended to hear nothing. Dismissing the redhead, she turned her attentions to the remaining duo. 'Now, who's next?' she queried.

Harold said nothing, simply dropping his shorts, turning around and bending over, as per instructions.

The cuts were delivered with a little less venom than the previous lot but stung, nonetheless. Harold was surprised by the woman's power, considering her apparent age and frailty. He accepted his punishment, wincing but silent. When she was done and had dismissed him, he pulled up his shorts, buckled his belt and left the office. After he'd closed the door behind him, he stood with his ear against it to see if he could hear how Tommy was faring. He heard a cry similar to the redhead's after each whack. When it was over, he left the building and waited for Tommy outside. When Tommy emerged, Harold was thrilled to see that he hadn't shed a tear, although he was rubbing his backside furiously with both hands.

'How'd you go?' asked Harold.

'Mar fish' was Tom's odd reply.

Harold had no idea what it meant. It was a term that Tom had learned from his father, a returned soldier who had picked it up in the Middle East. Tom didn't know what language it originated from but would always use it to indicate that things were okay, under control, hunky-dory.

'Beat you back to the tree,' Harold challenged. The two mates raced off, leaving behind them all thoughts of their first scrape together, its stinging results and any lessons that it might have taught them.

6
Getting to Know Tom

Have no friends not equal to yourself

Confucius (551–479BCE), *Analects*

Harold won the race but Tommy chased him tenaciously all of the way. They sat together quietly for a moment, regaining their breath. It was a clear, almost warm subtropical winter's afternoon and the run had left them sweating.

Harold scrutinised the expansive orphanage property for the first time. He was surprised to notice that the wooden paling fences around the circumference of the estate were only about four feet high. The first thing that crossed his mind was how simple an escape would be. Apart from the road that led up from Banyo, there was nothing but bush and farmland beyond the perimeter of the property on all sides, as far as the eye could see. The Catholic Church, as usual, had bought well, purchasing the land cheaply. The 300-acre parcel was on high ground compared to the surrounding countryside.

He noticed that next to the dormitory in which he'd slept, there were two other dorms. Along the fence at the back of the property were two barns and a neat, small brick cottage with a chimney. About half a mile away from where they sat, there were another two dorms and a large group of girls and some small boys running and playing. He couldn't make out what kind of games they were playing and didn't really care, because he knew the kind of games girls favoured. They weren't his cup of tea.

He asked Tom why the girls were so far away. Tom didn't raise his eyes as he spoke, just stared at the ground in front of him.

'They keep us all in different sections,' Tom explained. 'There's four separate lots. There's the real little ones, they're called the infants. Till they turn five, the nuns look after 'em in the convent.' His voice lowered slightly. 'I've got a little sister called Edith in there. We were brought here together and they split us up straight away. They never let me see her. I don't know what harm it'd cause anyone but they just won't let me. I hate it. I think about her all the time. I s'pose she must be all right, otherwise they'd tell me, wouldn't they?' It was part question, part wishful statement.

Harold had no idea. He shrugged his shoulders. Tom was pensive for a moment, still staring at the ground, leaning forward, his elbows resting on his knees, fingers intertwined. Harold struck the same pose.

Tom continued. 'When the kids turn five, all of 'em, boys and girls, move over to that section over there, with the big girls,' he said. 'The boys stay there until they turn ten and then they're brought over here. The girls all stay where they are.' He returned to his private agony: 'I wonder if I'll be able to see Edith from here when she turns five and moves out of the convent and in with the big girls.' He lifted his head and stared longingly in the direction of the girls' dormitories.

Harold, sensing his new mate's torment, felt he should say something but he couldn't think what. He wasn't any good at this sort of thing. He placed a tentative arm around Tom's shoulder. It was a comfort to Tom, a simple comfort the like of which he hadn't felt from anyone for a long time.

Suddenly, both felt a little awkward. Harold removed his arm and decided to change the subject. He noticed two nuns pacing slowly back and forth, in opposite directions, along a concrete path that ran down the middle of the playground. There was no evidence of conversation or even acknowledgment between them as they passed each other. Each was holding her big rosary beads and seemed to be praying. Each kept a close eye on the children as they paced and prayed.

'Why are those nuns praying out here, Tommy?'

'Dunno. They do it all the time. Must drive 'em barmy, I reckon,' Tom replied.

Both were now looking at the ground again as they spoke.

'Jeez, it'd be hot with all that stuff on that they wear, wouldn't it?' Harold observed.

'Yeah.'

'Why are the sheilas and us blokes kept separate?' he asked. Tom looked at him sideways, surprised at the naivety of the question. 'Dunno.' That would do for the time being, until Harold worked it out for himself.

'Lunch wasn't much good. Do we ever get anything decent to eat?'

'At least we do get lunch on Sundays. We don't get it any other day. The closest we go to getting something decent's when someone from the gov'ment or some archbishop comes visiting. Then they put a decent spread on. That's not too often, though.'

'Shit, eh.'

'Yeah.'

'What time's tea, then?'

Tommy momentarily glanced at Harold as if he was odd. 'Teatime, of course – whenever they tell us. You never know what time things are gonna happen round here. They just do. There's no clocks around and most of the kids here can't tell the time anyway.' He didn't mention that neither could he. 'Anyway, what difference does it make? It's never any good.'

'Do we get much for tea?' Harold didn't worry as much about the standard of the food as he did the quantity.

'Nuh. You wouldn't want too much of what they give you, anyway. It's usually a chunk of bread dipped in milk. Sometimes you can taste a bit of sugar in it. Sometimes we just get it dry. Every now and then we get some stew but it's not much good. Fridays we always get fish, some kinda fish.'

It wouldn't be anything new for Harold to be hungry, but he had been hoping for something better.

'In the afternoons in summer they bring around a big tin full of water. It's real clean water, too. We're allowed to have a cup each.'

'Shit eh.'

'Yeah.'

'What happens after tea?'

'Nothing. We have to go and get our nightshirts on and kneel beside our bunks and say the rosary with the dorm sister. Then we all go to bed.'

'More bloody prayers!'

'Yeah.'

'Shit.'

'Does anyone ever run away?'

'Some have tried to. It's not a good idea. They always track 'em down and they're sent straight to the reformatory. No second chance.'

'Reformatory, eh.' Everybody knew that reformatories were like gaols for kids – just as tough as adult gaols, just as mean. You didn't want to end up in a reformatory.

'Yeah. And you probably didn't notice last night, but they lock all the doors and windows at night in the dorm – doesn't matter how hot it gets.'

By now most of the boys who'd been playing cricket had either tired of it or lost interest because they couldn't get a bat. There were about a dozen aficionados remaining. By process of elimination, they'd established themselves as the best.

'Come and see if we can get a hit, Tommy,' Harold suggested.

'Nah.'

'Ah, come on.'

Tom was reluctantly persuaded. 'Aw, okay, but I can't play cricket.' He failed to mention that he couldn't play anything else, either.

For some reason, this time Harold got to bowl straight away. Before long he was batting. He'd been right: none of these kids could get him out. He had never had a lesson in batting, bowling or catching – but he was blessed with a good arm and eye, fast hands and excellent coordination. He never missed at least a few days' play of an important match at the Gabba cricket ground, though it took all of his substantial skills to get in for nothing, via one of several secret entry points. It gave him the chance to closely study the styles of his heroes. He had a gift for being able to copy their stances and techniques.

When Tommy took his turn at bowling, his absolute lack of ability became a source of fun to the others. He sprayed deliveries in all directions but he kept on trying to get them at least somewhere near where he wanted them to go. Eventually, almost miraculously, he managed to bowl a ball on line with the stumps. Harold missed it purposely and it hit its target with a clunk. Tommy couldn't believe it. Now the only problem was that it was his turn to bat. He had absolutely no idea what to do and when the first boy bowled the ball at him, much too quickly, all he could think was to get out of the way of the thing as hastily as possible. He dropped the bat and retreated swiftly to a position of safety, causing uproarious hilarity among the fielders.

He was out first ball, clean bowled, to Harold's grave disappointment. Tom saw the look on his face and it only made him feel worse.

'Don't worry, Tommy,' Harold said to him. 'I'll give you a few pointers when we get a chance. You'll be right.'

Tommy wondered if Harold really knew what he was getting himself into, trying to turn him into any kind of sportsman. All he could respond with was, 'Yeah, okay.'

The boy who had bowled out Tommy took his place at the crease. Harold took up a fielding position in the outfield. One of the bowlers proved himself to be particularly useless, pitching balls halfway along the wicket. Finally, he delivered a ball so extraordinarily ordinary that the batsman, gleefully taking full advantage, smashed the thing with all of his might, sending it sailing well above the heads of the fielders and clattering onto the roof of one of the dormitories, from which it rolled away, to the rear of the main building. It fell to Harold to fetch the missile, which he proceeded to do, muttering all of the way about the class of cricketer with whom he'd been saddled.

He located the ball beside the open back door of the nuns' kitchen. As he retrieved it, his attention was drawn to a young nun seated at a table, an infant nursing eagerly, greedily at her breast. He stood momentarily stock-still, silent and stunned, unsure whether to acknowledge her or ignore her. His preference was to disappear into thin air. He hadn't consciously uttered a sound yet somehow the nun became aware of his presence and raised her head. Tears were streaming down her face. Her eyes were filled with grief and resignation so vivid and sad that Harold would recall it all his life. He attempted to speak – to offer something by way of consolation or sympathy – though he little understood the source of her obvious torment. Words failed to materialise. His throat dry and thick, he decided it was best to say nothing, and walked away silently to return to the playing field. He thought that he should keep the incident to himself and hoped the nun would do the same. He was never to hear anything about it or see the young woman again. In later years, he would often think about her and hope that she'd achieved some happiness in her life.

The players were called in at two-thirty, by now chatty, dirty and sweaty. Harold made friends with most of the boys with whom he'd played. His willingness to mix it with Alby, the redheaded kid, had gained the other boys' respect and they admired his cricketing prowess.

The chat ceased as soon as they entered the dorm. Following Tom's lead, Harold changed back into his good clothes.

'Don't we get to play for the rest of the day?' Harold asked, trying to keep his voice down.

'Nuh. We have to get dressed up again and line up around the front of the convent,' Tommy whispered. 'They call it the Procession of the Blessed Sacrament. We have to do it every Sunday. Don't ask me what it all means, I haven't got a clue. We just do it, then get unchanged again.'

'Shit, eh.'

'Yeah.'

The procession was performed by a group of reasonably tidy little girls and grubby, uninterested lads, all inwardly wishing they were back out in the playground again. It was a ritual that involved slowly marching and singing hymns, with hands clasped in supplication, from the front of the convent to the chapel. There, a brief Benediction was performed and the Eucharist – the Blessed Sacrament – was installed in its resting place in the tabernacle on the altar. Then, the children marched back to the front of the convent and were dismissed. It all took about half an hour. Harold, Tom and the rest changed clothes once more and returned to the field of play, none any the wiser about what had actually transpired during the proceedings, or why.

Before long it was Harold's turn to bat again.

7

Telling Maggie

Our remedies oft in ourselves do lie,
Which we ascribe to Heaven

Helena, *All's Well That Ends Well*, William Shakespeare

Maggie had to hold the cup with both hands to guide it to her lips but the tea tasted good and its warmth soothed her stressed and raw nerves. She had taught Mollie well and it was exactly as she liked it – hot, milky and sweet. Mollie sat opposite her, filled with concern for the mother she loved whose behaviour of late had become so erratic. Nellie was at her side, her red eyes bearing testimony to the fact that she'd been in tears for most of the day since her brother had been taken away.

Maggie could barely stand to look at her Nellie, in her sadness. It wasn't as if she hadn't dwelt many times on the situation she had created. She had no idea why, since she'd become addicted to drink, she sometimes found herself actually despising Harold; why at times she had thought of him as a millstone weighing her down. At her lowest ebb, she had even wished him dead and gone. Acceptance of her pregnancy with Harold had not come easy for Maggie. She was forty-eight then and had thought that she was past her child-bearing years. The kind of happy and fulfilled sex-life that she still enjoyed with Patrick was frowned upon by the Church – God meant sex for the purpose of procreation only, according to its doctrine – and she found herself feeling self-conscious as her shape began to change. She imagined that the sniggering whispers of the self-righteous parishioners of the church that they so conscientiously attended were all directed at her.

Now, the boy had become more than just a responsibility. The demands of her addiction were manifold and one of the side-issues was that she in fact had come to hate her son. He was the one indisputable hindrance to her achieving her subconscious aim, which was to indulge and perhaps eventually destroy the one whom she now despised more than any other – herself.

She momentarily felt ashamed of herself for such thoughts and tried to dismiss them from her mind. As she returned the cup to its chipped saucer, Maggie's attention was distracted by the state of her hands – hands that were once so beautiful but were now blotched and wrinkled. Her nails, previously well cared for, were now cracked and ugly. 'Oh Mollie, what am I going to do?'

It was difficult for Mollie to know where to begin. Maggie might be reduced to alcoholism but she was no fool. Surely, she must be aware that she needed to overcome her addiction first of all and then her other problems would largely solve themselves.

Mollie had stayed with Nellie overnight and Maggie had arrived home just before dawn – inebriated, ill-tempered and untidy. Despite her surprise at finding Mollie there, she hadn't argued when her eldest had suggested she go straight to bed. In her intoxicated state, and for once not intent on attacking her son, it hadn't occurred to her that he was missing. When Maggie had awakened and cleared her head, Mollie had told her about the fate of her youngest child.

Mollie answered slowly, thoughtfully. 'I suppose the first thing we must do is to go to the police station and make inquiries. James will be able to give us the information we need. Then we must arrange for Harold to be released as soon as possible. He must be in a terrible state, poor little thing.'

'Yes, yes, that's what we must do,' Maggie agreed. 'I'll be ready in a minute.' She stood but the room swam about her and she slumped back into her chair. 'Oh dear,' she muttered.

'Perhaps it might be better if you wait here and I go down,' Mollie suggested.

Maggie thought for a moment, then agreed once more. Indeed, confronting the local police may not be a good idea, at least until she could call to mind what she'd done during her latest binge.

'May I come with you, Mollie?' Nellie asked, not wishing particularly to have to stay with her mother at the moment. She was as desperate as Mollie about the situation and wanted her brother back home.

Mollie hesitated momentarily but noticed the look of pleading in her sister's expressive, dark eyes. She understood, and nodded. 'Yes, of course, sweetheart. Put on your shoes and we'll be away. We'll be back as soon as we can, Mum.'

Nellie clasped Mollie's hand firmly as they walked some one hundred yards to the Woolloongabba police station, a two-storeyed brown brick building that backed onto the cricket ground.

After telling her sister to sit on the bench just inside the entrance, Mollie stood quietly at the counter for a moment, waiting for one of the two policemen on duty to notice her. The older of the two – a balding, middle-aged, slightly overweight man, tall and dressed in full uniform – rose from his desk. She knew him. He was Senior Constable Dwyer.

He walked over, saying, 'Yes, Miss, what can we do for you?' His voice was restrained, almost quiet, surprising Mollie. Most of the police that she'd come across were much brighter, more outgoing.

'Good afternoon, would Constable James Fraser be here at the moment, please?'

The policeman faltered, glancing quickly at his workmate. He seemed somewhat stunned by her query and Mollie instantly noticed his awkward hesitancy. He regained some of his composure. 'You're Miss Mollie Fingleton, aren't you?' He recalled that she'd visited their station before on behalf of her mother and he'd often heard young Fraser speak of his respect and affection for her.

Mollie felt a chill in her blood. 'Yes, James and I have been close friends for most of our lives. Is there anything wrong?'

Nellie was now at her side. Mollie placed her arm around her shoulder. Something warned her that they might not want to hear the policeman's response.

Dwyer came around from behind the counter and invited them both to sit with him on the bench. His tone was hushed, confidential. 'I know that his family have all been advised of this, so I'm permitted to tell you the dreadful news that, tragically, Constable Fraser lost his life last evening while on his way home from work. He was killed when struck by a goods train at Nundah station, I'm afraid.'

Mollie cupped her face in her hands and whispered, 'Oh, dear God.' She struggled to restrain herself from crying. It was unseemly, she felt, for a lady to cry in public.

Nellie could not summon the same kind of restraint. Her romantic wish had always been that Mollie and James might someday marry. She found herself sobbing again. The two sisters hugged one another tightly, each trying to console the other.

Suddenly, it occurred to Mollie that Harold may have been with James at the time of his death. 'Is our brother all right?' She almost screamed the words.

'Yes, yes, he's safely ensconced at St Vincent's.'

Mollie and Nellie each breathed heavy sighs of relief.

'That's the only good thing about the entire sad affair. James's death occurred after he'd delivered your brother to the orphanage.' He dropped his eyes as he spoke. 'A good young fellow and a good policeman, with a promising future in the force, was James. He'll be hard to replace around here. We shall miss him.'

He looked at the other officer for confirmation. 'Aye, that we shall,' he agreed.

Dwyer suddenly seemed to become self-conscious of his display of sensitivity. With a shrug of his massive shoulders, he stood to his feet and assumed his normal, authoritative posture. He cleared the remorse that had gathered as a lump in his throat and asked, 'What was it you wanted to see James about?' He had a fair idea, of course, of the reason for their call.

His return to his normal duties caught Mollie momentarily by surprise. Through the haze of her grief and shock, she sought the words that she needed. After a moment, she spoke slowly, ever so softly: 'I . . . I hoped, Constable, that you might be able to tell me what we have to do to get Harold back from the orphanage. I am sure there's been a grave error. As I confirmed with James when he came to collect Harold and as I think you well may know, he lives just around the corner with his mother and Nellie here.'

'Yes, I am aware of his circumstances. I'll have to check some paperwork. Give me a few minutes, will you, please?'

A figure appeared at the door. It was Maggie. She'd gathered herself together rather remarkably, washing her face and combing her hair. She had obviously determined that she had nothing to fear from the police at the moment.

'Good afternoon, Mrs Fingleton, I know why you're here. Please take a seat with your daughters and I'll be with you in a moment,' said the constable.

Maggie sat down between her daughters and Mollie turned and told her the awful news about her dear friend. Mollie's stoic façade dissolved then and she sobbed deeply. Nellie again bubbled over at the sight of her sister's tears. The motherly instinct, so completely absent of late, returned to Maggie and she hugged her children, rocking them slowly back and forth, her arms firmly around their shoulders. For her daughters, it was a comforting reprise of the kindness and loving warmth their mother had always been capable of prior to their father's death. 'There, there, my darlings, it's a terrible, terrible thing but we'll get through it. We've managed it before and we'll manage it this time as well.'

The moment and the mood were broken by the sound of a cough. 'Excuse me,' Dwyer said, embarrassed to cut in on this private moment between them. He spoke directly to Maggie. 'Look, Mrs Fingleton, you'll have to contact the State Children Department about this matter. The office is closed, of course, until Monday morning at nine o'clock. I'm afraid this is all the information I can help you with. It'll be up to the director to decide what's to happen with the boy. To be perfectly frank with you, having read the relevant report, you may have your work cut out for you to get him to release your son to you. You know the address, don't you?'

Maggie and Mollie both nodded. The state government buildings were at North Quay, in the city. Thanking the policeman for his assistance, the three of them left.

Kitty was waiting for them when they arrived back at Stanley Street, having called to check on the children. Over several cups of tea, they brought her up to date with the dismal turn of events.

Maggie would need to be sober and coherent when she called to see the director the next morning. A bath and some food, if she could keep it down, would help, followed by a good night's sleep.

8
School Days

*For lust of knowing what should be known,
We take the Golden Road to Samarkand*

James Elroy Flecker (1884–1915)

The pain in his jaw kept Harold awake for most of the long, solitary night and he welcomed the arrival of the morning – and breakfast. Today it consisted of the usual: bread with milk and sugar. His mate warned him not to scrape the bowl loudly with the spoon 'or they'll clout you'. The soggy repast proved a blessing of sorts: he need not chew very much. It did little to fill his stomach, but it was more than Nellie and he had gotten to eat most mornings for the past couple of years. After some metallic tea, breakfast was over.

As they filed out from the dining room, Harold decided that he desperately needed to tell someone about his painful jaw. The tall, skinny nun at the doorway had a kind face; he'd take a chance on her.

'Sister, I think me jaw's broke or something. It's real, real sore.'

'Where's it sore?' The nun was Sister Mary Alphonse.

'Just here.' Harold pointed to the left side of his face, near his ear.

Looks proved deceiving. 'Let me see.' She took his face in both hands and pushed her right thumb heavily against his left jaw.

He screamed in agony. 'Aw, shit!' he cried. Although he felt his knees weaken, he managed to remain upright.

'You may quit the bad language, you foul-mouthed boy,' said the nun and slapped his face, compounding the awful pain he was already suffering. This time he momentarily blacked out and fell to the floor. His head spun wildly. In the distance, he thought he could hear someone say, 'Get up, you cowardly fellow. You only have a toothache.' He responded to the instruction, regaining his feet and some of his composure. The reverberating voice continued, 'At lunch time you will go and wait in the hall outside the Mother Superior's office. When she has time she will see to you.' The words echoed through his semi-consciousness and he managed somehow to scramble them together in their correct sequence.

At that moment Tommy motioned urgently for him to

follow, so he attached himself to a group of boys. They headed out of the building and across the yard to a paddock at the rear of the property. The fresh air helped him to fully regather his wits and he saw that the group numbered about fifteen in all.

He was about to get his first taste of the kind of work the boys were expected to learn to do. The ministry had set up a system to teach them how to handle farm animals and perform farm chores so that if any of them were fortunate enough, they might be fostered out to a farming family somewhere in the state. Harold looked on as the others worked together to muster a small herd of cows through a gate and into the larger of the two barns he'd seen from a distance previous the day. He'd never seen cattle before and they were much larger than he'd expected. He gave them a wide berth, unsure of the disposition of the beasts. Once inside the barn, the boys tethered them by rope collars to solid metal rings attached to one wall. A few of the group stuffed bundles of fresh dry feed into mangers for the cows to munch contentedly on as they were milked.

The eldest and longest-standing inmate of the place, a thirteen-year-old lad named Alfie, was in charge of the work party. His longevity at the orphanage meant that he was given more freedom and responsibility by the nuns. He told the other boys that he'd been able to access his file in the Mother Superior's office while doing an odd job for her one day and had learned that he'd been there since he was a few days old. His poor, single mother had died from loss of blood and lack of a doctor or midwife during his birth. No family could be traced by the authorities and so he was declared a State Child.

Alfie allotted Harold the task of collecting eggs from the chicken coop on the opposite side of the barn. Although he had no experience with this kind of thing, he reckoned it should be a simple enough job. He entered the coop with a wire basket and began to gather the eggs. He was taken with the warmth of them as he held them in his hand, and with how perfectly formed they were. 'Jeez,' he said, fascinated. He failed to notice the huge, haughty rooster off to one side that had been eyeing him from the moment he had entered his domain. Before Harold knew what was happening, he found himself under attack from the mad, flapping, pecking creature. He punched and flailed wildly at his assailant, all the while beating a rowdy, back-pedalling retreat. Getting out of the coop had become his one and only immediate consideration and the eggs he'd so far collected became casualties of his haste.

The commotion was a source of great and boisterous amusement for the others. Harold was the latest in a long line of newcomers for whom this particular trap had been set. He impressed everyone by acknowledging the funny side of his embarrassingly swift evacuation. He happily assisted with cleaning up the mess that he'd created, as the more experienced lads completed the job he'd started. One stood guard with a straw broom to ward off the rooster while the others did the rest. Some of the others scattered copious handfuls of corn for the chickens to eat.

Another group was busy milking. The sight of the warm, creamy liquid squirting from the cows' udders into spotlessly clean white enamel-coated five-gallon buckets made the boys drool. Harold asked innocently, 'Can we have some?'

His query was greeted with a chuckle and a wise half-grin from Alfie. 'If we want a thrashing we can,' he replied. 'Every time we have some, they seem to know. Dunno how. Reckon one of these blokes must be a spy.' Harold surveyed the members of the group, wondering who it might be, if indeed there was a spy at all. Nobody seemed a likely candidate. It might even be Alfie himself, Harold thought.

The milking finished, the cows were returned to their grazing paddock for the next few hours. Another milking party would repeat the entire exercise in the late afternoon. Each of the boys helped carry the heavy buckets back to the main kitchen, desperately careful not to spill any of the precious contents. All then returned to the barn to undertake their next, more arduous morning chore.

Each collected an axe from the barn and made his way across the property to an adjoining heavily wooded field, there to spend the remaining time before school felling trees and chopping wood for use as fuel for the ovens in the bakery and kitchen.

A bell tolled for them to down axes, stack the wood that they'd hewn inside the big barn and get ready for school. They were allowed a cup of clean water each and a visit to the lavatory before lessons began for the day.

There were four classrooms, three of which were each shared by several grades. The thirteen-year-olds had the fourth classroom to themselves; they were studying for their certificate of leave, which, if successfully achieved, would gain them entrance to high school. There were always around eighty boys aged between ten and twelve at the institution, more than any other age group. There were fewer older girls because they were in great demand as nursemaids and kitchen hands on sheep and cattle stations and farms throughout the state. The classrooms were mixed, the girls seated at desks and most of the boys standing. There was never a hint of even the most casual interaction between them, for fear of their teacher's wrath. All of the children were white. Aborigines and children of other races were not given the benefit of the care of the Sisters of Mercy, at least not at this type of institution. They were put in missions instead.

Harold was dismayed to discover that Sister Mary Alphonse was to be his and Tommy's Grade 5 teacher. He was to learn that her previous cruel treatment of him was the norm. The woman simply had an angry streak.

School Days

It didn't take Harold and Tommy long to work out that one was no brighter than the other so cheating was going to be of little benefit to either of them. It was going to be a struggle. Truancy was not an option for Harold in this place. His earlier penchant for wagging school had seen him fall well behind the rest. Tough times lay ahead.

*

Mollie arrived at Maggie's place early that morning to ensure that her mother would be in a fit state to go to the State Children Department. She saw to it that Maggie was sober and tidy and that her hair was neatly brushed. Maggie wore her best dress, hat and shoes, worn down at heel though they were. Despite suffering the aftereffects of a lengthy drinking spree, Maggie managed to present as a comely and respectable woman. Mollie could not take time off work, so she gave Maggie firm instructions to inform her as soon as possible of the outcome. Maggie went on her shaky way, arriving at the department well before nine o'clock.

At around eleven, after putting her case as sincerely as she could and making some desperate promises the likes of which she could not possibly have hoped to keep, she left the director's office shocked and disappointed. The regulations stated that she could not retrieve her son at short notice but would have to prove that she was a fit and proper mother capable of providing appropriate support and care for him. She was given a mandatory period of six months to demonstrate her capability to measure up. She would have to report to the police station daily to exhibit her sobriety and, of course, if she breached any law she would set her case back substantially.

Maggie was waiting outside the factory gate when Mollie finished work. Mollie was equally shocked. How was she going to explain to her brother that she couldn't keep her promise to him?

As she often did, she consulted with her parish priest, Father Maroney, taking Maggie along. The Church was capable of pulling powerful strings and Mollie knew it.

Their meeting with him that evening served only to set them further back on their heels. Under the circumstances, there was not a thing he could or would do. He had long been aware of Maggie's shortcomings as a mother to her youngest child and had wondered privately why the boy had not been taken away sooner.

The next viable plan was to visit St Vincent's as soon as possible, to speak with the sisters there and to see Harold and explain the situation to him.

*

The classroom was chilly and the children, who were shoeless, covered one foot with the other alternately for warmth. After brief prayers for guidance and forgiveness of their sins, work began. The first lesson of the morning was arithmetic. If Harold had one weakness greater than any other, it was arithmetic. He could see another thrashing looming large in the future. His foreboding proved accurate.

Sister Mary Alphonse was middle-aged. Like her Mother Superior and many of her sister nuns, she had been sold by her parents to an Irish nunnery as a teenager. Like most of the others, her life experience amounted to constant prayer and sacrifice, the convent lifestyle and her teaching. A posting far away from their loved ones and the green, fresh fields of their homeland, to an arid, hot continent on the other side of the world, epitomised what was for all but a few their grim destiny.

She announced that she was about to introduce her students to multiplication and division of fractions. Harold's and Tommy's eyes met in blank stares. They didn't even understand fractions. How were they going to learn to multiply or divide them? 'This is gunna be nice,' Harold whispered, or so he thought. Somehow, he was heard by everybody and giggles rippled across the room, especially among the boys. The thrashing he had been expecting was upon him earlier than he'd reckoned on.

Alphonse's weapon of choice was a strip of bamboo an inch wide and three feet long. She deployed it upon her victims' hands, legs, rumps, backs or shoulders, whichever suited her at any given time.

The nun, who saw ignorance and lack of ability as laziness and a personal affront to her teaching, spent the entire class in a blaze of fury. The morning's study was interrupted by one thrashing after another for the unfortunate children. All of the while his jaw continued to cause Harold awful pain, the ache exacerbated by the chilliness of the room and his cold feet.

Not soon enough, it was time for lunch break and Harold was dismissed to hurry to the Mother Superior's office. After a brief wait in the hallway, he was called in.

'I'm told you have a toothache, Master Fingleton.' She noticed that the left side of his face had begun to swell since she had last seen him. 'Let me see.' She gently placed her hand under his chin and asked him to open his mouth. Harold flinched at her touch, bracing for another jolt of pain. He needn't have worried. This woman, at least, was no sadist. He opened his mouth as wide as he could and she looked inside. There was discernible redness on the lower left gum line. She stroked the side of his face, again as gently as she could, and could feel that there was heat in it. She guessed an abscess was forming. Her experience told her that worse pain was yet to come for Harold.

'I want you to go to the first aid room. You'll find it at the end of the hall near the kitchen. See the sister in charge there and tell her that I sent you. Explain your problem and she will give you something to ease the pain a little and then you may return to your class. The dentist will see to it on his next visit here in a fortnight. In the meantime, see the first aid nurse at lunchtime every day.'

'Thanks,' said Harold, grateful for her kindness.

'Thanks, Mother,' she insisted.

'Thanks, Mother.' He was not in the mood to argue over niceties.

He found the first aid room and the nurse recognised his ailment as readily as had the Mother Superior. She took a small bottle from a cabinet and removed the cap. It contained a fluid with an extremely sweet, almost pungent aroma. Using a small swab of cotton attached to a probe, she daubed the fluid onto his affected gum. He felt a burning sensation at first and then the entire left side of his face became numb.

The agony gradually ebbed away as he walked back to his classroom. It was replaced with a warm, almost comforting throb, which also gradually eased. The room was filled with children but there was no sign of Alphonse. Strictly speaking, the lunch break applied only to the nuns. The children were left to busy themselves with schoolwork. The smaller ones practised their writing or reading skills. The others worked at arithmetic tables, read some history or wrote essays. A monitor, one of the older girls, was left in charge. Her only duty was to report to the teacher anyone who'd misbehaved or had even spoken during the teacher's absence. There was always someone to tell on. Some of the older, braver boys would simply leave the room to play in the yard, returning to face their comeuppance when lessons resumed. They didn't relish their punishment but, maturing into young men, they wanted to demonstrate a little defiance, despite the consequences. The lads reckoned that the exercise of belting them helped the nuns to digest their meals. After the punishment was meted out, studies resumed, with the following hour devoted to Christian doctrine.

Harold and Tommy enjoyed the stories of the saints, especially the martyrs. The gruesome methods used to put some of the martyrs to death held a macabre fascination for them, as it did for most small boys. Harold's knowledge of his catechism was negligible. His religious instructor, Sister Mary Alphonse, would see to it that it improved. The ultimate aim of the Sisters of Mercy was for the children to develop into good and useful servants of the Church and after a lifetime of devotion, gain entry into the kingdom of Heaven. If they had to resort to extreme violence to achieve this end, so be it.

With the doctrine session completed, they moved on to conventional studies, including English, history (mainly

British) and geography, until four o'clock. Sister Alphonse became less excitable as the day progressed. Harold and his mate reasoned that she'd simply worn herself out during the morning. She resorted to throwing things, sometimes pieces of blackboard chalk, more often the duster, which was a small slab of wood with felt glued to it. Whichever child was her target was required to return the object to her and this resulted in at least two cuts with the bamboo. Harold and Tommy were impressed with her aim: she rarely missed her mark. Harold reckoned she wouldn't disgrace a men's cricket team, so good was her arm. He wondered if she could bat.

9
Visiting the General

And never a saint took pity on my soul in agony

Samuel Taylor Coleridge (1772–1834)

'Idle hands are the devil's tools' was a popular adage among the nuns. Certainly, it seemed to the orphans, they all voiced it often enough. They managed to organise enough work to keep potentially idle hands as busily occupied after school hours as before. All inmates did their share.

By far the children's most unpleasant chore was getting rid of the tiny, biting bugs that infested their bedding and made them all itch. This task was undertaken once a week, on Saturdays. The children carried their palliasses outside and dusted them with a white pesticide that stung their eyes.

Then they shook the mattresses to release the powder – and, hopefully, the dead bugs.

Laundry, sewing and clothing repairs were designated as girls' work. The other major tasks that fell to them were the bathing and feeding of the infants in the main building. The older boys used scythes and reaping hooks to cut any overgrown grass on the property. The bakery that supplied warm, fresh bread daily for the nuns' table was operated by the older boys and girls. It was housed in the brick building that Harold had noticed earlier, between the two barns.

The dairy developed into quite a productive enterprise and the nuns gradually enlarged the size of their herd. Any surplus milk or cream was either sold to shops in neighbouring suburbs or made into cheese, some of which was also sold. An elderly, ruddy-faced, good-natured gentleman, Mr Potter, would arrive at the orphanage once a week aboard his horse-drawn cart to collect the dairy produce for delivery to the orphanage's customers. A group of three or four boys was selected to assist the old fellow in stacking the cart and then unloading the heavier cans at various drops along the way. He was a popular visitor, as he would teach the lads how to harness and even to take the reins and steer his passive, ageing workhorse. Thus it was a great adventure, providing the boys with a brief, welcome change of environment, if only for a few hours.

Deliveries regularly took far longer than they should. Unbeknown to the nuns, the trip usually involved a stop-off at a hotel or two, where Mr Potter would excuse himself to 'wet his whistle'. When he returned to the cart, he would usually require assistance to remount the thing. Small boys, even three or four together, are of little help to an overweight, drunken cart driver whose balance and strength have temporarily abandoned him, so this exercise would degenerate swiftly into high farce, with much giggling and raucous laughter by all concerned, including Potter.

Darkness begins to gather at about five-thirty in midwinter in the subtropics. All work had to be completed by then. Then the children were finally permitted use of the lavatories again, having been denied the opportunity all day. After a quick sluice of the face and hands and a small mouthful of clean water if they were quick, it was time for dinner.

At the conclusion of the meal, it was bedtime – but not before a long-winded hour of prayer, most of which comprised the rosary. The dormitory sister would recite the first part of each Hail Mary and the children would chorus the second part. The Lord's Prayer, between each decade of Hail Mary, would be said by all in concert. Any child seen not to be concentrating or praying devoutly enough could expect to receive a clout at any moment. Harold and Tommy did their best but if they closed their eyes in mock piety, they were in grave danger of falling asleep where they kneeled, lulled by the drone of hushed supplicant voices. It was the longest hour of every day for them and staunch willpower was demanded for them to see it through.

One night, sleep came swiftly enough for Harold at first but he awoke when his jaw ache escalated and became excruciating. He got out of his bunk and walked quietly about the dormitory in the darkness, his left hand pressed gently against his face. He imagined that walking around, together with the warmth of his hand, seemed to allay the pain a little. Many of the boys were restless, some weeping, calling softly for their mothers. All Harold wanted was some relief from his pain. First light found him exhausted but thankful for the passing of the night. Morning lessons dragged on and he counted the minutes until lunch break, when he could once again visit the nursing sister for treatment with some of her miracle cure. The secret, delicate mysteries of fractions were no nearer his intellectual comprehension than they'd ever been as he waited at the door of the first aid room for his turn to see her.

*

Maggie again called at the State Children Department, this time to find out when she could visit the orphanage.

Visiting the General

St Vincent's monthly visiting day happened to be that coming Saturday and Harold was allowed two visitors, so long as they had a pass signed by the director of the department. Permission was granted, the pass was signed and Maggie set off with Mollie to St Vincent's on Saturday morning.

They arrived at ten a.m. By now the swelling on Harold's face had grown more obvious still. His mother and sister were startled by the sight of a pale, sick boy, obviously in terrible agony and barely able to greet them even though he was happy to see them. He was pleased with his mother's sobriety, but his immediate concern was telling them about his state of pain. 'Please, Mum. Please, Mollie, see if you can get 'em to do something about me jaw. It's killin' me, fair dinkum.'

Mollie hurried to the Mother Superior's office, leaving Maggie to cradle her son's head in her lap. It had been so long since he'd been cuddled by his mother and he wished he could fully savour her gentle stroking of his head and the calming solace of the moment – but in his pain, it wasn't possible.

Mollie sat across the desk from the senior nun. Both women sat straight backed, Mollie with her gloved hands in her lap.

Mother Brigid spoke first. 'Good day, Miss Fingleton. What may I do for you today?' The thought crossed her mind that here was a mature woman who, on the surface, looked capable of having done more to protect her young brother from what had befallen him. Politeness and protocol prevented her from addressing the issue.

Ever respectful, Mollie quietly replied, 'I am Harold's eldest sister, Mollie, Mother Superior. His mother and I are visiting him for the first time today, as you would know. We are very concerned with the state of Harold's face. It's very swollen and I wonder what caused it and if you are aware of it.'

'I am certainly aware that he has a toothache, Miss Fingleton, but it is a few days since I have seen the boy personally. We've been treating him with a daily swab of oil of cloves. It normally keeps any pain at bay for almost twenty-four hours. We have a dentist who visits us every two months. He's due in a week or so. I'm sure he shall see to your brother's problem then.'

Though normally deferential to priests and nuns, Mollie mustered as much daring as she could and argued her point. 'Mother, would you do me the personal courtesy of seeing him again, please? I am concerned mostly with the fact that he may have some kind of infection. I have seen one such infection before. The heat and the swelling in his face seem to me to be abnormal.'

'There is nothing more we can do at present, Miss Fingleton. As I have already pointed out, the dentist will not be here until next week.' Then, relenting: 'However, if it will make you feel better, I shall send for the boy and we shall inspect him together.'

'Thank you, Mother. I'd appreciate that very much.'

The Mother Superior rang a small bell, summoning a sister to her office. 'Sister, go and fetch Master Fingleton and bring him to me, please.'

The nun emitted a barely audible 'Yes, Mother' and, with an abbreviated bob, hurried from the room. Before she had returned, Mollie had been brought up to date with Harold's conduct during his short stay at the institution. She was not at all surprised to learn that he had been 'difficult to control'.

'I have to admit to a liking for the boy's innate boldness,' said the nun. 'He has impressed me as a natural leader but it is that very boldness that we are forced to subdue. Such a boy can cause us a great deal of trouble. Because he has the potential to lead, other boys may follow his example. It is essential that we maintain control of the children's behaviour at all times and this can lead to what may be construed as cruel treatment of them. Our choices are rather forced upon us, I'm afraid.' She expressed her point with all honesty, fully confident in its validity.

'Mother,' Mollie said, 'Harold has had very little joy in his life in the years since our father died. Our mother has become dependent on alcohol to the extent that she's been rather neglectful of him and has often harshly mistreated him. I've done what little I could to protect him from her.' She hesitated momentarily, unsure of the truth in the words that she'd just uttered. 'It would be a terrible thing if he were to suffer more of the same whilst in your care.'

The nun cast her eyes briefly downwards. Then, straightening the folder that lay before her on the desk, she countered defiantly, 'We are supplied with a case history, when one is available, of each child that we receive here. Your brother is no exception. Neither is he an exception to have suffered the way you say he has. None of the children whom we are charged with nurturing, educating and raising has had it easy – otherwise they wouldn't be here in the first place. Nevertheless, we must maintain decorum and certain standards lest we end up handing over control of the place to the children themselves. Obviously, that would not do, would it?'

'Of course not, Mother,' Mollie meekly conceded. She had already surprised herself by pressing the Mother Superior. It was normally not within her scope to argue the point with a priest or nun.

A rap on the door heralded Harold's arrival.

'Oh, dear Lord' was as much as Mary Brigid could manage to mutter when she saw the lad. Shocked and alarmed by his unhealthy pallid hue and the increase in the swelling since she'd last seen him, she acted swiftly. To the young nun who had brought the boy to them, she said,

'Sister, go immediately to collect a nightshirt and dressing gown to fit this boy.' She turned and reached for the telephone on the wall behind her. Hastily she arranged an ambulance to transport him to the General Hospital.

An operation revealed that one of Harold's lower back molars had been snapped well below the gum line. The resulting infection was on the verge of entering his bloodstream. It had become more virulent because, with the lack of good nutrition over a lengthy period, Harold's immune system had been weakened. The surgeon removed the tooth in two pieces and Harold remained in hospital for the next five days.

His mother and sisters visited him every day. They spoiled him with the kind of attention that he hadn't had for a long time and it made him feel a little uncomfortable – even slightly embarrassed. Kitty brought him lollies every time she visited. She didn't have to. As far as Harold was concerned, she had to bring only the warmth and sweetness that was so much a part of her nature.

The hospital food, though famously distasteful to most, was delicious and plentiful to him. He regretted having to leave.

Tommy was excited to see him when he returned to St Vincent's. 'I wondered what happened to you. They wouldn' tell us nothin'.'

'I was in hospital. They had to cut me gum to pull out that sore tooth I had. I'm glad they did it – it was killin' me.'

Harold wasn't really aware of the profound truth of his statement.

Maggie's sobriety, tidy appearance and kindness had given him hope for the future. At the hospital, she had told him that he had to spend the next five or so months at the orphanage but that she was determined that he'd be home for Christmas. He was disappointed that he wasn't going home right away but thankful that, unlike most of the others in the orphanage, he could dare harbour expectations of a relatively early release.

10
A Brief Release

It is true that liberty is precious –
so precious that it must be rationed

Nikolai Lenin (1870–1924)

The inmates of St Vincent's orphanage were subjected to a regimen of repetition and harsh discipline. The treatment was meant to bore and demean them and stifle misbehaviour. It was considered essential to the institutionalisation process. When the process was successful – and it proved to be with very few exceptions – it led to the peaceful and cohesive running of the place. The end result was an orphanage housing mostly sad, frightened and harassed children whose abiding fantasies revolved around absent or imagined families and an ordinary life beyond the constraints of this place.

Harold inevitably became the leader of the handful of boys who rebelled against authority. The price he had to pay was that most often he was the one blamed for any misconduct. He organised most of the games and also the fist fights, which occurred in the far reaches of the grounds at frequent intervals. In his view, these had to be conducted fairly, as one-on-one contests between boys roughly of the same age. No bullying of smaller boys was permitted. If one or more of the combatants disagreed with these rules or procedures, they could always take it up personally with him. Few took that option. There developed a clearly defined pecking order, with Harold, the best scrapper, at the apex. One of the perks of such a position was that there was no longer any argument about who should be at the front of any queue. Harold was therefore able to have a clean bath every Saturday night, his fill of clean water to drink when he hopped in and a bar of soap to lather himself with.

The priest for the parish of Banyo, Father Clancy, visited the orphanage regularly to minister to the nuns and children alike. Clancy heard Confession on Saturday afternoons. This supposedly gave the children as little time as possible to again grievously sin before Sunday morning Mass, thereby ensuring that their souls were pure and unblemished for the reception of the Blessed Sacrament of Holy Communion. The Christian doctrine lessons to which they were subjected daily were mostly wasted on Harold and Tommy and they understood little about the difference between venial and mortal sin. They decided it was more expedient during Confession simply to invent some sins, perform their allotted penance and move on with their lives. Harold, on a few occasions, confessed to being guilty of committing the sin of adultery. He wondered why the priest seemed faintly amused when he did so.

A handsome, portly gentleman in his early forties with prematurely silver hair and a ruddy complexion, Clancy was a sports fanatic, quite at ease with a cricket bat in hand. He could always be found at the football, and on Friday nights at the professional boxing at Brisbane Stadium. He particularly enjoyed the races and regularly received a slightly better price from the bookmakers, most of whom were eager to gain any possible advantage in their battle with the punters, including potential blessings from a higher power.

Clancy provided a sympathetic ear when Harold told him about a plan he and his mates had hatched to construct a concrete cricket pitch for the older boys. The priest recommended that they be allowed to go ahead with the scheme and it was viewed favourably by the Mother Superior, who no doubt was inspired by the adage about idle hands.

Work commenced on the first day of November. There wasn't a great deal of excavation necessary, as the base of the pitch needed to be only about twelve inches deep by six feet wide by a chain, or twenty-two yards, in length. The hours of daylight were lengthening as summer approached, so every afternoon after they had completed all their chores they dug the pitch, under Clancy's supervision. There was no shortage of manpower and the boys attacked the job with great enthusiasm.

Father Clancy made inquiries with a local builder about the best way to construct the formwork for the cement. The builder, a good Catholic man, happily donated enough lumber for the formwork and decomposed granite for the base. Within a fortnight, the base had been laid and the first batch of cement mixed and poured. At the end of a month, with the concrete levelled and cured, the pitch, while not as aesthetically pleasing as some purists might like, was ready. Appropriate blessings were conferred by Father Clancy and play commenced in the first of many competitive and rowdy matches.

*

Maggie had been living for some time in a house in Bridge Street, Fortitude Valley, with Nellie and her son Patrick. He had gone to work at a sheep station outside Cunnamulla, west of the Great Dividing Range, at age fifteen, just before Maggie had begun to drink. Having returned for a brief holiday, he decided to stay long enough to see Harold home from Nudgee. Towards the end of Maggie's probationary period, Senior Sergeant McCarthy of the Valley police reported to the

State Children Department that she had 'remained sober for the past six months'. With Maggie's pension, the board she received from Patrick and Nellie, who were both working, and assistance from a Salvation Army member named Mary who had befriended Maggie, the senior sergeant was convinced that a 'comfortable, safe home was awaiting the lad'. He recommended that 'the boy be released from St Vincent's immediately and returned to his mother's care'. The minister of the department, satisfied that Maggie had gained control of her drinking problem, gave his approval.

On Christmas Eve 1920, Harold left the orphanage. He was excited about the prospect of spending a Christmas with his family, especially a sober, gentler Maggie. He was disappointed that Tommy would not be allowed out for the day to be with them. Mollie had assured them that Tom would be returned safely on Boxing Day but the nuns would not relent. As he said goodbye to his best mate, Harold assured him that he would visit whenever he could. He was about to leave but paused for a moment. Turning towards his friend, he asked, 'Aw, by the way, Tommy, what's your second name?'

'Thurman,' replied Tom. 'What's yours?'

'Fingleton. See you.'

'See you.'

Paperwork signed, he was officially released and walked with his mother down the hallway to the front door.

He noticed someone he hadn't seen since his first night at the orphanage and had all but forgotten. It was Sister Teresita. She was now much thinner than he remembered her to be. Clothed in her full nun's garb, she was seated, slumped, in the hallway outside the main office, in an uncomfortable-looking wheelchair. Her eyes were motionless and stared glassily at the floor. Harold didn't know that she'd suffered severe injuries that night and had been unable to communicate with anyone since.

The feeling of sheer elation as he took his first few steps from the orphanage and began the walk down to the railway station took Harold by surprise. There seemed to be a different smell to the air. He chatted incessantly all of the way down the hill to the station. He wondered out loud about his brothers and what they were doing. Was Nellie going to be there when they got home? And Kitty?

The train ride was more enjoyable than Harold's previous one with James. He spent most of his time kneeling on the seat at the open window but would from time to time sit back down beside his mother. She would place her arm around his shoulder and he would experience a sense of security and calmness that had become strange to him in recent years. Each time he returned to her side, Maggie noticed that he seemed to sit closer, as if to regather the confidence in her that he had lost. The next day promised to be the best one of his life, he thought. Mollie, Nellie, Kitty and Patrick would all be there to spoil him, there would be presents and Maggie would cook some delicious food. He would be able to enjoy the most wonderful Christmas ever.

At one o'clock on Christmas morning, the police found Maggie by the Brisbane River nearby Breakfast Creek and arrested her for drunkenness and foul language. She was imprisoned later that morning at Boggo Road Gaol.

The same day, Harold was returned to St Vincent's. He was just over two weeks short of his twelfth birthday.

Because it was Christmas Day, the police officer in charge of delivering him back to the orphanage made an exception and permitted Mollie to accompany them on the train journey. Along the way, Harold thought to ask after James. He'd been disappointed, but not surprised, that the policeman had not kept his promise to visit him occasionally.

'Oh, Harold dear, I don't know how to tell you, but I suppose I have to. I'm afraid James had an accident and was killed the evening you went to St Vincent's.'

Her brother's reaction was a shrug of his shoulders and a brief, barely audible 'Hmmph, another one.'

Mollie didn't quite understand. 'What do you mean, darling?'

Though he'd liked James, it surprised Harold that his death caused him to feel this way. Looking blankly at the passing scenery, not really seeing any of it, he tried to understand why he felt such a sense of loss. After a short time, he mused: 'Why do things always turn out like this? People you like either die or treat you like a dog.'

'Oh, Harold, I don't know' was all Mollie had to offer in consolation.

Harold said nothing for the remainder of the trip. When the police officer reminded Mollie that she'd have to bid her brother goodbye at Banyo station, she felt coldness in Harold's response. She observed something in his eye that concerned her deeply, a look that she'd never seen before, almost of blankness. The vitality that had always danced within them had gone dormant. As he and the constable faded into the gathering dusk on their way up the long hill to the orphanage, he looked back at her and managed a somewhat dismissive wave. She waited for the train that would transport her back to the city and prayed solemnly for her little brother.

11

Out for Good

I only ask to be free. The butterflies are free

Charles Dickens (1812–70), *Bleak House*

Harold arrived back at St Vincent's in time for Christmas lunch but before he could join the others he had to go through the readmission process. It didn't involve ablutions again – although he no longer really cared that much anyway – just a brief visit to Mother Brigid's office.

Many years of dealing with orphaned, abandoned or mistreated children had taught the senior nun much about their psyche. She knew that almost invariably they assumed all blame for the situation in which they found themselves, rather than blaming an irresponsible, abusive or alcoholic parent, poverty or difficult circumstances. Most of these children believed that it was something in their own personality or behaviour that caused their abandonment.

Many decided that they were simply unlovable. Some, resigned to their fate, would never come to terms with taking responsibility for their own lives, would forever seek approval and guidance and be forever dependent upon others. A very small percentage would manage, through innate determination and optimism, to absorb fate's unkindnesses and achieve happiness and success or at least a regular life. Others would rebel stubbornly against any and every attempt to control or to discipline them. They would spend most of their lives in conflict not only with law enforcers but with society in general.

She'd learned the tricks to reading their body language and facial expressions. That was why the boy who now stood before her gave her cause for apprehension. The lad whom she had dismissed into his mother's care only the day before had always exhibited a carefree, animated eagerness, a charming zest for frivolity and mischief. Even in the face of punishment, he had always retained that cheeky attitude. In a matter of hours, the cheekiness and bravado that she'd warmed to over the preceding six months had gone. They had been replaced by something else and she recognised it quickly. Eyes that had been full of light and colour had dimmed and now were downcast. When he did look at her, it was as if he were not really seeing her. His chin had taken on a different set. There was a curl to his upper lip that gave him an aura of utter impudence. She sensed that the lad who had returned to her care was going to be even more of a handful than he'd been before.

She told him that she was sorry to see him back, sorry that things hadn't worked out for him. Immediately she wondered why she felt the need to console him. It was not her normal practice to indulge the children in this fashion. Perhaps it was the season. She went on to tell him, though, that he would be expected to settle back into the routines that he'd become used to prior to his short release. Although he must be very disappointed at having to return, nothing would change; he would still have to obey the rules.

He nodded and mumbled a barely audible 'Yes, Mother' and was dismissed to join the rest for lunch to celebrate the birth of the Saviour.

Each of them received a small portion of ham, a baked potato, a scoop of a mushy vegetable mixture and some watery gravy. The metallic tea was replaced with raspberry cordial – weak but a treat nonetheless. Harold joined the others eating the meagre repast but could think of nothing but the feast he was missing and the company of his brothers and sisters, even perhaps a Christmas present or two.

He was completely demoralised. Why? Why had his mother let him down again?

*

Mother Mary Brigid's fears were quickly realised.

Harold, already having proven his willingness to solve any problem with aggression, now engaged in bouts of bullying and fighting almost every other day, and was punished accordingly. A stint at Westbrook Reformatory beckoned, were it not for the infinite patience of the Mother Superior. Others like him had been sent to the reformatory in the past and it was mystifying to the sisters that the same fate had not befallen him. It was not their place to question the Mother Superior's authority, however, and none ever did – after all, they had taken vows of prayer, chastity and obedience.

Mother Brigid recognised Harold's conduct for what it was: the result of a program he had undertaken of self-loathing and self-destruction, no different from that of other boys before him. His commitment to the program was unrelenting. He took pride in displaying to the other boys the innumerable welts and bruises he received as punishment for the trouble he caused. They were to him badges of courage and to the other boys, fair warning of what they might expect if they took him on. He gained the respect of some, the fear of others. So belligerent was he that even older, stronger lads were no match for him. It was nigh on impossible to defeat an opponent who was not only capable but also feared neither injury nor punishment. Tom would try to talk some sense into him, to save him from himself, but it was a waste of time.

As corporal punishment was not successful, the nuns used other measures. They denied Harold the few pleasures that most of the other children enjoyed, such as an occasional trip by coach to the beaches at Sandgate or Redcliffe, watching a performance one day by clowns from a touring circus and even the rare good meal the boys were fed in the event of a visit from a government minister or an archbishop. They barred him from games that they knew he loved, such as football and cricket. He hated to miss out but would not relent; their punishments served only to deepen his conscious resolve to misbehave.

Towards the end of his second six months at the orphanage, Sister Brigid's resources of patience and perseverance had evaporated. Arrangements were being put in place for his removal to Westbrook when notification was received that Maggie had once again convinced the authorities that she had recovered from her alcoholism. This time she had gained employment as a laundress.

In late June, Harold went to live with his mother and Nellie, this time in Boundary Street, near St Paul's Terrace, in Spring Hill, right next to the CBD of Brisbane. He was enrolled at the state-run Central Practising School, which catered for the children from the mostly poor families in the area.

Harold was biding his time for the next eighteen months to pass, when he would turn fourteen, be discharged as a State

Child and be able to get a job and fend for himself. Everything depended on him staying out of trouble and Maggie doing the same. If he acted up or if she couldn't remain sober and keep her job, he would be returned to Nudgee – or worse still, and more likely, be sent directly to Westbrook. He kept himself busy by swimming, playing Rugby League for the Fortitude Valley Diehards and cricket for any team in the district that needed a player. He still loved his cricket but these days he was happiest when he was playing Rugby League. It was the perfect avenue for the release of aggression and the sometimes fierce body contact suited his nature perfectly. He was fast, a willing, tenacious defender and a natural at centre play. Soon he was earmarked by his coaches for future first-grade and representative honours.

Maggie managed to surprise everyone, including herself, by staying off the drink. With the passage of time she had come to reasonable terms with the loss of Patrick and regained some of the self-respect that had deserted her for the previous few years. She became popular with the Sisters of Mercy nuns at All Hallows Convent for her small kindnesses, such as baking fancy cakes and biscuits to sell at their regular school fetes. A pair of nuns would visit her on most Sunday mornings after Mass for tea and conversation. Harold made certain that he was off the scene when they were due. He'd seen enough of the Sisters of Mercy to last him quite a while.

*

Mollie had become close friends with a nursing sister, Lucia Arena, five years younger than she was, and they'd taken a flat together at Bowen Hills, close to the Royal Brisbane Hospital, where Lucia worked. Lucy, as Mollie called her, was from a wealthy Italian family who had come to Australia via the USA in 1900, when she was four years old. Her personality was much stronger than Mollie's. Bright, cheerful and intelligent, she was renowned for her ability to demand and achieve cooperation from the most difficult and unruly of patients. She was a career nurse, who during some of the fiercest battles of the First World War had served close to the front lines in France, tending to injured and dying Australian soldiers. In time, the two women decided to move to Sydney together.

Peter had joined the army in 1915 when he turned eighteen and was initially stationed at Townsville for training. Exhibiting values at odds with those of his youngest brother, he embraced the discipline of the army. Apart from the small matter of a charge of going AWOL on one occasion to visit his girlfriend in Brisbane and seeing the inside of an army stockade for a month as a result, he enjoyed the lifestyle. He fought in and survived the Great War and upon his discharge in 1919, he undertook an apprenticeship as a painter and decorator. He eventually gained his trade papers and, in 1920, married his longtime girlfriend, Dulcie. They were to have three children – Laurie, Beatrice and Claude – before Dulcie died of pneumonia in 1930, aged twenty-nine. Harold's and Peter's personalities were totally different and they never became close, even in later life.

Harold had had virtually no contact with Patrick since he'd gone to work in western Queensland. Pat learned to shear sheep and made a good living. Like most shearers, who moved from one sheep property to the next as their services were required, he was a casual, hard-drinking, easy-going fellow. He would return to Brisbane for extended periods and remain until his money ran out or he tired of the city life – and then he would be off to the country again. Harold saw a little more of him during these visits and missed him when he went away again. Despite his apparent shiftlessness, Patrick was devoutly religious and when he turned twenty-one in 1924, he achieved a lifelong ambition by becoming a missionary with the Catholic Church. He was packed off to New Guinea to work among the indigenous people, who were perceived by the Church to be heathens in desperate need of conversion to the Catholic faith. Some of them were head-hunters, some cannibals.

Patrick disappeared at the age of twenty-two, never again to be seen or heard from, either by family or Church.

Nellie worked for a few years as a barmaid, eventually marrying a man named John Morgan when she was thirty.

They had a son, whom they named Jack, and enjoyed a happy life together, until she died at the age of fifty-two from tuberculosis, the disease that subsequently was to claim Peter's life as well, in 1957.

Margaret and her husband, Fred, eventually returned to Brisbane from Charleville. Fred set up his own building business and they bought a home at Greenslopes, in Brisbane's south, where they started a family and lived well. Fred was a rambunctious, opinionated character, not popular with the Fingletons, especially Harold, so the Schoenwalds were infrequent visitors to the Fingleton house. In 1948, Margaret died from lung cancer and, within a year, Fred remarried.

*

Harold spent much of his spare time at Mick and Kitty's place and often slept over. Kitty was the only person really capable of calming the beast within the boy, the only person with whom he felt completely safe and at ease. She was placid and willing to quietly spend time talking with him about his experiences at the orphanage, his emotions and his ambitions; and she was able to get through to him and help him control his moodiness and temper. Her tenderness brought a composure to Harold that no one else could bring.

Mick was always pleased to see Harold and made him feel at home. And Harold loved to train with Mick, a fitness devotee. Before and after work and at weekends, Mick operated a gymnasium, where he earned a good reputation as a trainer of boxers, cyclists and other sportsmen. He also had an arrangement with the Gabba police to take under his wing any troubled young bloke that they considered worthwhile persevering with. He would work them hard. His premise was uncomplicated: he'd send them home exhausted, much more likely to want to go to bed than hang about the streets and pubs, getting into strife. He would assure his charges that if they cooperated with him, he would at least get them fit and better equipped to handle any situation they might find themselves in, with the police or otherwise. While it wasn't an entirely infallible system, it worked for many of the young men.

Mick was well aware of the extreme edginess of Harold's personality. He saw that other boys Harold's age were no match for him in sparring sessions. Harold was simply too aggressive, too competitive, too fearless and too competent. He would spar furiously, unable to come to grips with the idea that sparring was meant merely to be a fitness exercise.

Mick saw the need to spend more time on him, to teach him well. His student's aptitude was evident. He had a natural athlete's balance and brilliant speed of foot and quickly mastered the exquisite art of rope-skipping, with all of its tricks. His timing was sharp and he carried good strength in his punches with both hands. His right cross, in particular, was extremely powerful and delivered with what Mick liked to call 'snap'. Mick's main problem was in convincing the lad of the importance of a good defence – the ability to move cleverly and evade punches. And Mick knew that Harold, with his belligerent attitude and angry streak, was going to need to become very skilled at that – otherwise he would find himself on the unpleasant end of hiding after hiding when he went up against bigger or more skilled blokes. So Mick set about teaching Harold all he knew of the finer points of self-defence. It took a while for the message to sink in. A couple of well-placed clouts and a broken nose from Mick speeded up the process. Once learned, the lessons were never to be forgotten.

A recently retired middleweight, Snowy Hill, trained at Mick's gym to retain some strength and condition. He decided to become a trainer in his own right. His own boxing career had been less than fruitful but he fancied that there was big money to be made at the training caper. Indeed, eventually he became one of Australia's most famous and successful fight trainers. He approached Harold, through Mick, and offered to train him. Snowy's offer was steadfastly rebuffed by Harold and Mick, who both saw professional boxing as a mug's game.

Mick wasn't about to allow his young student to become anyone's mug. He hoped, somewhat futilely, that the skills he had passed on to the youngster would be used predominantly for self-defence.

12
No More Pencils, No More Books

Liberty means responsibility. That is why most men dread it

George Bernard Shaw (1856–1950)

The youngsters of the inner-city suburbs of Spring Hill and Fortitude Valley in the 1920s were a free-spirited, tight-knit, tough lot. With few exceptions, they were very needy, made needier still by the fact that they came from big families and their meagre finances had to stretch to feed, clothe and house many brothers and sisters. Birth control was not a viable option because most were Irish Catholics and the Church precluded all but abstinence as an acceptable method. Most families rented free-standing timber houses known as Queenslanders, a style unique to the state. They usually had wide verandahs and high ceilings and were set upon tall wooden stumps to take advantage of any breeze that might spring up in the late afternoon in the hot, humid summers. Most had yards out the front and back.

There was little in the way of organised entertainment for young people. There were some police sporting clubs, mainly football and cricket associations for the boys.

Girls were given scant consideration. They were expected to learn to cook, knit, sew and keep a tidy house, their ambitions revolving around a future husband and children. They should enthusiastically tackle the task of producing offspring, to contribute to the growth in population of what was still a very young country. Major changes in attitude to the value of women in society were still many decades off but small steps were being taken. In a mighty breakthrough, Edith Cowan had become the first woman to sit on a state legislative assembly when she defeated the incumbent attorney-general and won the seat of West Perth in the 1921 Western Australian elections.

In suburban Brisbane there were also a few women bucking the status quo. Dora May Milner was one of them. A slim, pretty and congenial girl, she was possessed of a broad mind and an outrageous sense of humour. She went almost everywhere with her brother, named Harold but better known as Jock because of his love of horseracing and gambling in general. Their mother, Annie, was a strict disciplinarian and she let Dora go out with Jock mainly to keep him under control. Dora was popular with all of her brother's mates, especially Harold William Fingleton. He had been smitten with Dora from their first meeting.

Harold had been expelled from the Central Practising School for brawling and displaying a total lack of respect for his teachers. The authorities gave him one last chance to stay out of Westbrook Reformatory and he enrolled at Fortitude Valley State School. Dora was a couple of classes below him and Jock. Harold would go to outrageous lengths to try to impress her. He was prepared to risk life and limb, performing daring dives from the high board of their favourite swimming pool, as long as Dora was watching. His skill was minimal, but his courage was unquestioned. She effectively stilled the turmoil in him to the extent that he managed to remain at school until the end of his fourteenth year, earn his discharge as a State Child and finally have the opportunity to get a job and earn some money of his own.

Mick, who'd been promoted from the position of signal maintainer to maintainer-in-charge, could have arranged a job for him on the railways but figured that Harold might not be suited to it. He called to see an elderly acquaintance – a man named Mr Wills, who owned and operated a general store in Ann Street. The store happened to be not far from Patrick Street, where the Milners lived. Mr Wills had only one interest in his life and that was his grocery business. His wife had died several years earlier and he opened the store at six o'clock sharp every morning of the week. Nobody ever saw him away from the premises, where he lived in a flat at the back. He told Mick that he'd been considering hiring some help, so was happy to give his young brother-in-law a start.

Harold's chores around the shop included serving customers when things became busy, keeping the place swept, dusted and tidy when it wasn't and doing the odd pick-up or delivery. He was also expected to stay alert on the rare occasions when the shop became crowded, because that was when stock had a habit of disappearing. Mills was too old to be chasing thieving louts up the street like in the old days and Harold's presence would make that unnecessary.

Or so he thought.

He was not aware of Harold's thinking on such matters. Not only was Harold unlikely to chase any louts up the street, he was likely to be one of the louts, if not their leader. Harold would pilfer things from the store and set them aside for his mates, including Dora and Jock, who would make a daily call at the shop to collect whatever Harold had been able to sneak aside for them. Dora, of course, received special treatment. There was often a small bag of broken biscuits waiting for her, and she and Jock would go home most afternoons happily munching on the proceeds of Harold's misdeeds. Much to her mother's chagrin, Dora and Harold were by now very close.

Wills had been in business a long time. He knew that

patronage should equate with takings. When they didn't, two and two quickly added up to four and for Harold, it was goodbye job and hello Mick's well-targeted boot.

It was the only time that Kitty had ever witnessed Mick angry. Everybody knew him to be calm and introspective, always in control. But he could not conceal his disappointment in the lad. Mick had earned his reputation through his integrity and honest, hard work. He didn't want Harold placing it in jeopardy by such behaviour and wasted no time in letting him know how he felt.

Such was his love and respect for Mick and Kitty that despite the embarrassment and indignity of his punishment, Harold accepted his medicine, suitably chastened, a lesson learned.

Mick was not one to dwell on things and once the matter was settled, he moved on. Realising that Harold was not best placed in a position of trust at this stage of his life, he and Kitty looked around for a tradesman who might need an apprentice. They reasoned, correctly, that it was not Harold's work ethic that was his problem.

Mick placed a sign on the wall of his gym and it wasn't long before a recently arrived Irish immigrant named Michael Moylan approached him offering to indenture Harold as an apprentice. Moylan, a painter and decorator of good reputation who often visited the gym to train after work, was not likely to stand for any nonsense from the lad.

Harold, who soon learned that Moylan was a meticulous tradesman and tutor, quickly adapted to the work and enjoyed it immensely. It provided him with enough money to pay his board at home and have some left over to enjoy himself in the company of his small band of mates. He was determined never again to disappoint Mick and Kitty in the manner he had done, and his willingness to turn out for work every day encouraged them.

He spent a lot of his spare time either with Dora or around the gym, helping Mick to keep the place tidy and training hard himself. There was never any shortage of sparring partners. Many a willing young man turned up at the gym because of Mick's reputation as a fitness conditioner. It was a sign of the times. The Great War was still a fresh memory and men who'd had the great good fortune to be too young to risk their lives in the armed forces often felt the need to test their mettle. There is no sterner testing ground than the inside of a boxing ring.

A civilised man rarely gets to experience what it feels like to stand in a small roped enclosure in possession of nothing to defend himself with other than his own fists while a complete stranger tries to bash him into submission or unconsciousness. Most who try their hand discover it to be beyond them – psychologically, physically or both. Young men would come and go at the gym, normally leaving a little wiser than when they came, in possession of a useful gift: a gauge of their own limitations. Only the very gifted possess the combination of skills necessary to succeed at the boxing caper. But as Harold and all of the others learned, there is one quality more important than all of the rest. That quality is courage – guts – intestinal fortitude. Call it what you will, it is something that cannot be taught. Although courage alone will not carry a boxer for his entire journey, once he climbs aboard for the ride, he will certainly need it to pay his way.

For those who persevered, Mick would endeavour to find a fair match. Not many of them would measure up even to amateur boxing class but there were plenty of what he called 'willing roosters' among his protégés. He approached one of the great showmen of the time, Jim Sharman, and proposed a business arrangement: he offered to provide shills for Sharman's travelling sideshow boxing troupe.

In Brisbane, the Royal National Agricultural Society annual show has always been referred to as The Exhibition – corrupted further still to 'The Ekka'. Of course there were the usual displays of farmers' oversized pumpkins and the judging of Friesian bulls, stud rams and stallions. There was heated competition for the first place blue ribbon in every category – from cakes to cats and dogs, arts and crafts to calligraphy. Some of those ribbons adorned the hearths of Queensland country homesteads for generations.

But the most popular attraction for patrons was always sideshow alley. Some of humanity's oddest and quirkiest individuals were there for all to see – and then there were the shows. Spivs, conmen, tricksters, shysters, pickpockets all abided, in generous numbers. Many of the operators of the sideshows – the showies or carnies – were at least the second or third generation of their families to follow the unique lifestyle, and knew no other. The alley always seemed to be situated in the dustiest section of the showgrounds, so the carnies invariably gave the impression that they had been estranged from a bar of soap for far longer than they should have been.

For the mostly innocent, unsophisticated audiences of the time, it was a place of wonderment. Irresistible drawcards invariably included the bearded lady, the world's tallest man (one at every show) and fattest woman (also one at every show), the armless boy, the legless boy, even the headless boy. Patrons would enter in awe to inspect whatever thing of wonder had raised their curiosity and leave often in disgust. They may have feigned amusement, usually realising that they'd been duped mercilessly, but most were too embarrassed to request a refund.

Somewhere nearby could be heard an intermittent rumbling, the rapid double beat of a bass drum. The rumble would continue for some minutes and suddenly cease. Onlookers who followed the sound to its source found themselves standing before one of the larger tents in the alley. Life-size paintings of great national and world boxing champions, present and past, adorned the outside. Lined up on a platform about ten feet above the ground was a grim-faced array of the toughest and most fearsome-looking men and youths imaginable, usually about seven or eight in number, one of whom doubled as the drummer. Of varying weights and shapes, some white, most Aboriginal, all decked out in boxing shorts, dressing gowns, gloves and boots, they stood ready for action. As the drumbeat ceased, out from behind a curtain appeared a dapper, rather distinguished-looking and handsome fellow with a megaphone in hand, which he raised to his mouth in order to challenge anyone in the crowd game enough to take on one of his fighters. Any challenger able to see out three rounds of fierce combat with one of his 'boys' would be paid a reasonable purse, somewhere in the vicinity of a shilling a round. On the surface, the idea was to shame some unsuspecting chap in the crowd into having a go. The dapper gentleman was Jim Sharman and this was Jimmy Sharman's Boxing Troupe.

The arrangement that Mick had with Sharman was a matter of expediency. Sharman could ill afford to spend too much time finding opponents for his boxers, as his prospective patrons might lose interest and move on to other attractions. Certainly, there was the occasional tough, genuine contender but not always. So Mick provided lads with some boxing expertise to stand amidst the throng and take up the challenge. Dual purposes were served: not only did the tent fill quickly with paying customers but it was also a lot safer to have challengers who were used to taking a punch. This way, there were fewer serious injuries and hospitalisations, everybody involved earned a quid, the audience got their money's worth and J. Sharman became a millionaire.

Young Harold was one who didn't need much encouragement to join in. The bumps and bruises were nothing new to him and the few extra shillings that he usually won came in handy.

13
Oats for Goats

Nature never deceives us. It is always we who deceive ourselves

Jean-Jacques Rousseau (1712–78)

Harold had not forgotten his mate Tommy. He was released from the orphanage and discharged as a State Child after some research was conducted, at the request of the Mother Superior, by officials at the birth registry. It turned out that he'd been born in February 1909, so by the time they let him go, he was closer to fifteen years old than fourteen.

Mick was happy to make arrangements to collect Harold's mate on the big day. Before long, Tom was at work as an apprentice mechanic and sales assistant at the bicycle shop where Mick purchased most of his cycling equipment for the gym. The fact that he was able to earn some money was a source of immense pride to Tom. It was the first time in his life that he'd even handled any. He'd need to be educated in how to manage it, so Mick and Kitty suggested that he give them a small portion of his wages for them to save for him, just as they'd been doing for Harold. It seemed like a wonderful idea to Tom and he agreed willingly.

It had been many years since Tommy had looked forward with eager expectation to what the next day might hold for him. His life was taking on some meaning and it felt good to finally be in a position to make some of his own decisions. His happiness would have been complete but for the fact that he yearned to know what had happened to Edith. Inquiries were made and it turned out that Edith had been adopted out soon after she and Tommy were taken to the orphanage.

The state's policy was to keep adoption details private, leaving Tommy no way to find his sister. Mick and Kitty made numerous nagging visits to the state minister's office to persuade them to make an exception for the lad's sake but their efforts proved futile. Even Maggie, with her extensive experience in dealing with the authorities, failed to achieve any positive result. The answer was always the same: 'Government policy on the issue is incontestable'. No information about the child's whereabouts would ever be released. It weighed heavily on all their hearts that Edith, having been separated from Tom at such a young age, would live her entire life without any idea that she had a brother at all.

Tom moved in with Harold at Maggie's place until he could afford to rent accommodation of his own. He was immediately welcomed into the corps of youths that roamed the streets of the Valley and surrounds in their spare time, creating as much mischief as possible, most of it relatively harmless but time-consuming for the local coppers to deal with. The rest of the gang included Albert 'Brickie' Farrell, nicknamed, of course, for his occupation as an apprentice bricklayer. Brickie was deaf in one ear, the result of a thrashing from his stepfather a few years earlier when he'd tried to stop him from subjecting Brickie's mother to one of her regular beatings. The bullying stepfather had fled the family home when Brickie, having finally grown strong enough, gave him the hiding that he'd had coming. Brickie was a tall, freckly, sandy-haired fellow, as game as they come and very useful in a stoush.

There was the ruddy-faced Jack 'Irish' Radley, whose family had arrived from the Emerald Isle five years previously. His mates found his rapid-fire brogue all but impossible to understand, especially when he became excited, which was often. When he lost his temper, his face would redden dramatically and he'd unleash the most fearsome tirades, seemingly forgetting to even breathe, saliva spluttering in all directions. It didn't help when his rants made the rest laugh uproariously, as they sometimes did. Each of them eventually perfected the art of very convincingly assuring Irish that he'd made himself understood. It just wasn't worth the angst it caused him – and everyone else – when he had to constantly repeat himself. Harold loved his mad aggression and the utter fearlessness he possessed. Short and stocky of stature, it was generally accepted that Irish would rather have a fight than breakfast.

John 'Johnno' Mann was a builder's labourer who lived up on St Paul's Terrace with his ageing parents. A big, cumbersome fellow, his normally jolly exterior belied his willingness to mix it up with the best of them when called upon. His passion was politics and he was given to lengthy dissertations on the issues of the day, with minimal prompting.

There was Jock and, of course, the ever-present Dora, the only girl regularly and openly welcomed into the company. She brought to the group a semblance of balance and good sense, which fortunately was often enough to dissuade the boys from their more dangerous or stupid or illegal prospective adventures. All of the boys enjoyed her company, not only because by now she was Harold's girlfriend and they didn't really have any say in the matter, but also because she provided a sympathetic ear for their many personal troubles. She possessed a welcoming, freely offered and genuine feminine touch, often sadly missing in their lives. They could relax and be themselves around her and she was always careful to show a suitable level of amusement at some of their antics. She became inured to most of their foul language but never really approved of it and didn't hesitate to let them know when they'd gone too far. On the occasions when her mother didn't permit her to accompany Jock and the boys, left to their own devices the group found ways to busy themselves with riskier escapades.

They adopted a motto that had special appeal to them because few outside their circle understood its meaning. They were proud to chorus it often:

> *Oats for goats,*
> *Horses for courses,*
> *Tin hats for wooden heads,*
> *Uppercuts for mugs*

The first line referred to the oats, or porridge, that inmates were often served in gaol. If you were silly enough to get caught and end up there, you were a goat and deserved to be there.

The second was drawn from horseracing parlance. Expensive thoroughbreds race only on flat, high-maintenance courses to minimise their chances of injury. The inference was that you should never try to work outside your area of expertise. If you are a good pickpocket, for example, don't turn your hand to robbing banks – you'll probably make a complete mess of it and pay the price with your freedom.

They were in awe of the courage and resilience of the men who fought in the Great War and sympathised with the many thousands of families who had suffered terrible personal loss during the conflict. But it seemed to them that there had been an element of foolishness in the sacrificing of men's lives in defence, largely, of foreign lands. Therefore tin hats, the steel helmets that soldiers wore, were for wooden heads, not smarties, to wear. Occasionally, someone outside the group would point out that the Valley mob might be the real wooden heads. Opinions of that kind were not gracefully accepted and were better off not expressed.

The ultimate line was a simple fighting reference to the sneak punch reserved for the unschooled, the mug. Draw him in close and he doesn't even see it coming.

The motto summed up the street-smart, insolent youngsters' attitudes and grew to pervade every aspect of their swaggering, generally obnoxious behaviour. Their self-perception was that they were much cleverer than most. They dressed nattily, usually in three-piece suits with open-necked white shirts, and wore their felt hats jauntily to one side, as did the criminals depicted in their favoured gangster films. They were clearly marked for close attention by the police. What could safely be treated as mostly trivial and harmless today might, if unchecked, degenerate into serious criminal activity tomorrow.

There was a real belief among them that they were invincible and they didn't hesitate to demonstrate their toughness at every opportunity. Their collective antagonism surfaced regularly, with little provocation. It was as if there was a contest to see which of them could start the first fight. They never sought out defenceless individuals but there were enough other groups of tough youngsters around the place to take them on, so violent clashes were commonplace. Groups would arrive at local dances, sporting socials and private parties with the sole intent of creating as much havoc as they could.

Of course, alcohol acted as an incendiary device and the occasional brawl was the norm at most hotels on Friday and Saturday evenings. The lads weren't old enough to legally drink in hotels but sympathetic pub regulars helped them out by buying their drinks for them. Brawlers normally conducted their business outside on the footpath, because no one wanted to be barred by the proprietor of the pub. Once an outcome was arrived at, all were welcome – victor, vanquished and voyeur – to return to the comfort of the bar room to resume their tippling, until the next round of hostilities erupted.

The Marquess of Queensberry's rules were rarely consulted in these unpleasant situations. They were all-in fights. A proficient street fighter was a creature with unique instincts and expectations. Headbutts, knees, boots and elbows all formed part of his armoury. Inexperienced or faint-hearted contenders usually realised all too late that they were dangerously out of their depth and about to drown.

Harold, Irish, Brickie and Johnno more than held their own. Tommy and Jock would pitch in and throw their respective weights around but never achieved much, usually managing to be of only nuisance value. Harold reckoned 'neither of 'em could crush a grape'. Still, they were respected for having a go, somehow surviving to fight, or rather make pests of themselves, another day. One day Tommy and Jock had a major disagreement over a minor topic and fought one another. Tom won the fight but to the expert eyes of their mates, their display seriously lacked any of the exquisite fistic virtuosity that they themselves had at their disposal. The boys had occasional internal clashes like this but they were soon dismissed to the annals of history and forgotten, having no long-lasting effect on their friendships.

There'd always been a strong rivalry between cliques from neighbouring suburbs and the lads were very territorial when it came to the young ladies who lived in their respective patches. If a boy from the Valley invited a girl from New Farm to a football match or a dance, he'd better have his wits about him after he'd brought her home. There would be, without fail, a welcoming committee of New Farm lads waiting in the close vicinity. The Valley boy wouldn't be in danger of an attack by the entire group – that wasn't the way things were done – but he would be expected to fight one of them, usually a brother of the girl, or be exceptionally quick on his feet.

Most would stay and fight but the meeker and less capable would run. They would often turn to 'Fingo' for protection, knowing that the New Farm lads would not let the matter rest until it had been settled with fists. Harold enjoyed the status this earned him among his peers and would only too readily agree to be the proxy. His reputation as a willing and capable street fighter had grown and was bolstered further with each subsequent victory. His confidence in his ability escalated steadily. The less foolhardy of his prospective opponents simply backed down, demonstrating admirable good sense. The more reckless and uninitiated of them received their comeuppance. The police turned a blind eye to most of the territorial fighting unless a formal complaint was lodged by a member of the public, a rare occurrence. To most people, police included, it was all a bit of harmless tomfoolery – lads being lads.

But one Friday night Harold and his mates were taking part in a fight at the Shamrock Hotel when the police arrived. Senior Sergeant Jim McCarthy was delighted to find young Harold Fingleton in the midst of affairs, going as hard as he could. He'd often hoped he'd get the chance to catch up with the young troublemaker and give him the hiding he had coming. He and one of his constables swooped upon Harold from behind. Each grabbed an arm and then they drove him headfirst into the concrete-and-tile wall. The collision rendered him instantly unconscious. Another squad of coppers arrived just as Irish, fists flailing madly, was consulting with McCarthy and the constable in an attempt to settle the matter of the vicious assault on Harold. He and Brickie, hopelessly outnumbered, were swiftly subdued and placed under arrest. Johnno somehow managed to glibly talk his way out of that inconvenience, claiming to have been attempting to restore order. The unfortunate chap he had flattened moments earlier with a pearler of a left hook probably would have appreciated the opportunity to offer evidence to the contrary, had he been conscious at the time. Those still capable of doing so dispersed quickly, avoiding arrest. The coppers ignored the jeers and hisses of the large audience as they bundled five of the brawlers into a paddy wagon for removal to the watch house at North Quay for 'questioning'.

Harold hadn't moved since he'd been felled. Tom kneeled beside his pal, deeply concerned. 'You'd better get an ambulance for me mate here,' he said to the cops. 'I reckon he's hurt pretty bad.'

'Bullshit, he'll be right,' snarled McCarthy and then he told one of his constables to 'shove the bastard in the wagon with the others'.

Harold regained consciousness on the way to the watch house. The pain in his skull was worse than anything he could recall, even the septic tooth. By the time he'd been released on bail the following morning – to appear in court charged with affray on the Monday two days hence – he could barely open his eyes. Tom insisted on taking him directly to the General Hospital and Harold didn't argue. A couple of tram rides delivered them to the hospital at Bowen Hills, where an X-ray revealed the cause of his anguish: a skull fracture, for which he was admitted to hospital immediately. He would regularly suffer searing migraines for the rest of his days.

*

In the summer of 1925, Kitty died, three weeks after giving birth to twins. Only one, named Vincent, survived. After the babies were born, Kitty should have received thorough curetting but the nursing staff of the Women's Hospital failed to ensure she had the procedure and released her from their care too soon. She developed septicaemia and died at home, surrounded by her family and in the loving arms of her devoted Mick. She was twenty-five years old.

Mick would never fully come to terms with the loss of his beautiful Kitty. But he had always accepted his responsibilities head-on and readily assumed the duty of raising his three children in the manner that Kitty would have wished, as good Catholics and good citizens.

Dora was consumed by grief, having become very close to Kitty and having spent many hours helping her to care for her youngsters.

To Harold, this latest loss was beyond comprehension and beyond consolation. An even more fiercely intense and abiding rage began to surface within him. Dora had always been able to console him and control his moods but now he turned away from her and from his friends as well, with the singular exception of Tommy. He moved out of his mother's place and into a boarding house in Brunswick Street, a few doors away from the Shamrock Hotel.

He'd turned sixteen and was needing more and more grog to slake an ever more demanding thirst. Tommy, too, was developing a strong dependence on alcohol and was his constant drinking companion. They would usually take whatever booze they were able to get their hands on back to Harold's flat and drink it there. Tom generally knew when he'd had enough and would go home to the bedsitter that he now rented nearby. Harold, on the other hand, had inherited his mother's worst drunken traits and was incapable of recognising when he'd had enough. He'd drink on and would become more and more cantankerous. He was the worst kind of drunk: his aggression mixed with unpredictability produced sudden, instantaneous outbursts of violence. His behaviour began to make him unwelcome even among some of the drinkers who'd been supplying his and Tommy's grog. He found himself visiting some of the familiar wine bars where, as a child, he'd occasionally attempted to convince Maggie to leave. The regulars at these dimly lit establishments generally were older, confirmed alcoholics. They preferred to drink in solitude and introspection, the sadness of their lives shown respect by fellow drinkers and staff alike. The barkeepers at these places paid scant regard to his lack of years. His money was as good as anyone else's.

He would still turn out for work every day. To this end, he made the first few days of the week completely alcohol free. As difficult as that was for him, he managed to cope most of the time. As the weekend drew near, however, he'd begin again. Friday evening until Sunday was one long drinking session, spent usually in a morbid and maudlin mood. If he ran out of money, he'd seek out an easy target, niftily relieve him of his cash and then resume his binge.

He and Tommy became regular visitors to the Kedron Park pony racetrack, where there was no end of potential marks. The pony races were unique to 1920s Australia. Huge crowds of gamblers would flock to unregistered tracks to bet on up to fifteen pony races in an afternoon, usually midweek. These were not the social events that the Saturday races were. The pony races were patronised by the desperate and the greedy. All forms of skulduggery were practised. The animals that competed were normally smaller-than-average thoroughbreds or merely stockhorses. They were classed as ponies because they were no greater than fourteen-and-a-half hands tall, from wither to sole, while a normal-sized racehorse on average stands about sixteen hands tall. The ponies raced under a higher weight scale than their larger counterparts and it was not uncommon for them to compete in more than one event in an afternoon. Many of the most famous jockeys of the day were not too proud to take part, honing their skills on the tightly turning circuits. Bets large and small were placed and sometimes massive amounts of cash changed hands in the betting rings. But whatever the value of your wager, it was advisable to remain in close proximity to your bookmaker because some of them were desperate men, prepared to take risks beyond their means to settle. The punter expected to be paid after the race if his horse won, at the odds relevant at the time he placed his bet. A particularly unfortunate result for a bagman – when his settling commitments outweighed his holdings – could necessitate his sudden flight from the precinct, successful punters in angry and raucous pursuit.

Tom was a less-than-willing participant but he was a staunch friend to Harold. If his mate needed his help, he'd be there, no matter what. Tommy's role in Harold's pony-track scheme was relatively simple but his timing had to be good. Harold would stand among the shoving, elbowing crowd in the betting ring and deftly lift some gambler's wallet or wad of banknotes and quickly pass it on to Tom as he walked by. Then, casually, Tom would make himself scarce. Sometimes the mark might realise his misfortune almost instantly but if a calm and collected Harold was accused and searched, he would usually have no more than a few shillings in his pockets – and a most convincing air of innocence. He and Tom would then meet in a prearranged, secluded spot, divide their takings and promptly leave.

*

Tommy grew wiser about Harold's alcohol problem. Although he liked to drink with his mate, he realised that even he was not completely safe from Harold's mood swings when he was drunk. He learned to recognise the very early signs and would make an exit before the trouble started. To his mind, he wasn't really deserting his friend. He would be of little assistance to him in a fight anyway and would likely find himself on the losing end of a hiding. He wanted to survive to a reasonable age – and anyway, someone had to pay his mate's bail in the morning if the coppers became involved.

Young Fingleton was becoming more and more well known to the Valley police. He'd developed an altogether unreasonable, surly hatred for them and took every opportunity to demonstrate the most outrageous disrespect for them. They were accustomed to the traditional distrust and disdain displayed by the average Australian, a hangover from the past, but Fingleton's attitude and misconduct were becoming intolerable.

Jim McCarthy had retired and a replacement had been appointed at Fortitude Valley police station. He was an ambitious young man named Clark. Short and stocky in stature, 'Knobby', as he was nicknamed, was physically powerful and had a fearful reputation for toughness, which had earned him early promotion to sergeant-in-charge. He'd been given this difficult posting because of his no-nonsense approach to law enforcement. His mission was to get the Valley under control. His chances of further promotion within the force rested upon whether he succeeded. Clark made it clear to his fellow officers that he wasn't about to allow any bunch of young hooligans to stand in his way and was prepared to do whatever it took to complete his task. He and his constables would show no mercy to the hoodlums who had been running rampant for the past few years.

And as far as he and Fingleton were concerned, matters were destined to become personal.

14

Clarrie

A soft answer turneth away wrath

Proverbs 15:1

It seemed that no matter where Harold went, Clark or his constables were never far behind. It was not surprising, for Harold was targeting them with an aggravating, insulting new ploy. He would wait in ambush in a darkened doorway for a police foot patrol, normally two young officers, to pass and then pounce on them from behind, kick one or both as hard as he could in the backside, then race off, guffawing as he went. Inevitably, he would be captured and taken to the police station. There he received merciless beatings, usually with batons. It frustrated the police that he would never plead for them to relent. He would hiss and spit at them contemptuously, defying them to do their worst. Despite the fact that he had goaded them into it, he saw them as his tormenters, and his deeply ingrained hatred for them grew with each new beating. The injuries he suffered during these punishments, which might take weeks or months to heal, were more damaging to his body than to his defiant spirit. He was intent on proving to them that they could never force him to submit. Clark meant to prove that they could – and would.

Eventually, soon after having turned eighteen, Harold was brought before a court, found guilty of several counts of public drunkenness and assaulting police and, for his first offence, sentenced to six months' imprisonment at hard labour in Boggo Road Gaol. Clark was disgusted with what he considered to be a light sentence. He was confident that it wouldn't be the young criminal's last, however, and the thought consoled him.

Harold's conduct during his first few days in gaol was no less unruly than it had been on the outside. There was the small matter of his inability to grasp the concept of obedience to his masters. He simply could not conceive that any one of the baton-twirling, uniform-clad weasels known as screws could ever be his master. As a result, he spent most of his first fortnight in solitary confinement. If he kept being defiant he could expect more of the same. There was also the possibility of an extended sentence to consider. As much as it would have delighted him to bash any screw that came within reach, it became apparent even to him that good behaviour was a more advisable option.

As disrespectful of the law and its officers as he was, there was little that he could find to admire in the majority of his co-inmates, either. His allotted cellmate was a 35-year-old career criminal named Dowd. He was serving his seventh period of detention, this time for burglary, and seemed proud of it. Harold despised him at first sight. Dowd made the mistake of suggesting a sexual encounter and spent the following week in the prison infirmary recovering from his injuries. Harold copped another week in solitary for his trouble.

The incident did little for his popularity among the other prisoners, for certain protocols were expected to be followed by 'new boys'. His youth and good looks made him a very desirable mark for the more discerning, especially the long-termers. They would need to give Harold an education in the ways of Boggo Road.

He was wise far beyond his years, sure enough, but Harold was not prepared for what was to follow.

Exercise breaks were taken at the discretion of the prison governor, usually in the midafternoon. Few took advantage of the opportunity and most would simply laze idly about the vast yard that was within the prison's twenty-feet-high brick-and-concrete perimeter walls.

It was almost wintertime, the breeze was cool and the sun pleasantly warm. Harold found a relatively isolated, sunny spot and squatted quietly alone on the ground, his back against the wall. He closed his eyes for a moment. Suddenly, he heard the shuffling of scurrying feet and felt the searing agony of a kick to the left side of his body. Instinctively, he rolled in the direction of the kick and, despite his pain, was on his feet in an instant. He found himself confronted by Dowd and three others, none of whom he recognised. 'Get 'im!' one of them yelled. Harold wasted no time in assessing his chances. There was but one course of action open to him. He stepped forward, surprising the assailant closest to him with a perfectly timed right cross that laid him out cold. Before he could swing another punch, the other three, all big men, moved in, raining punches upon him. He called on all of the guile and defensive training he'd received from Mick, weaving his head from side to side and nimbly ducking about on quick legs, making as difficult a target of himself as possible, all the while throwing rapid-fire combinations of punches and generally doing whatever he could to stall the inevitable. He held his own for twenty or thirty seconds and flattened another of his opponents but after that he felt his strength waning from the sheer number of blows he'd absorbed. The punishment he was being subjected to was brutal. The screws were happy to ignore such beatings if it facilitated the swift compliance of newer inmates to the systems in place.

A deep, resonant voice away to his right caught his

attention and that of his attackers. 'Turn it up, ya team of mongrels, turn it up!'

The melee subsided as quickly as it had begun. The two who were still on their feet stepped back from the cornered Harold. The other two were unconscious. A very large prisoner now stood by Harold's side. 'That'll do. You've had ya fun, now piss orf.' To Harold's amazement and gratitude, the attackers immediately obeyed the barked instructions, however grudgingly. Mumbling incoherently under their collective breaths, they gathered up their slumbering allies and slowly shuffled away. 'And that'll be the end of it,' the big man warned them.

'Jesus, mate, thanks. I'd have done 'em anyway,' Harold ridiculously contended, 'but thanks. Who are you?' He suddenly became aware of a pain in his side – later he'd learn that one of his ribs had been broken in the onslaught. He grabbed his side and winced. His saviour placed a massive, comforting hand on his left shoulder. 'You can call me Clarrie, son. C'mon, let's have a smoke 'n' a bit of a yarn.'

Clarrie Weston was one of the most feared and respected hard men on the east coast. He was a registered painter and docker in his home city, Melbourne, where he had earned a reputation for leading and organising a fair proportion of the criminal activity. On the advice of a confidant in the Victorian police force, he'd taken a 'holiday' at Boggo Road until things cooled down for him at home. A minor gangster had disappeared suddenly, presumed dead, and he was wanted for questioning over the matter. The local cops cared little whether the warring gangs killed each other off – in fact it made their job easier – but they would go through the motions of investigating such an incident until the press lost interest or found another cause to trumpet in their newspapers. Interstate rivalries between police forces and simple lack of communication between them would ensure that Clarrie could hide out in Queensland then safely return home after a reasonable amount of time out of the spotlight. He'd been given a brief sentence at Boggo Road, under an alias, for assault and battery.

The two men sat and talked quietly. Clarrie was impressed that Harold didn't have much to say. He liked the fact that the youngster was more prepared to listen than talk. A closed mouth could be trusted. It turned out that Clarrie had been asked to look out for the young fellow by Geoff Davies, a wharfie, also from Melbourne. Harold had struck up a friendship with him at the Wickham Hotel when Geoff was visiting Brisbane for a time to escape the cold of the Melbourne winter; they were to become lifelong mates. Geoff had done some 'hard' jobs for Clarrie and even a short gaol term on his behalf, for an offence that Clarrie had committed while he was on parole and could ill afford another pinch.

Under Clarrie's protective wing, Harold's security was

assured and the remainder of his time in Boggo Road passed uneventfully, however slowly. Maggie, Tommy, Irish, Brickie, Johnno and Jock were regular visitors during his incarceration and Mollie travelled from Sydney to see him as well. Dora, however, was forbidden by her mother to visit him.

After his release, on a Saturday morning, he stood for a moment outside the prison as the steel gate clanged heavily behind him. He'd walked only a few yards but somehow, just as it had when he'd left the orphanage, the air smelled cleaner and sweeter on the outside of the prison walls than on the inside. A rush of adrenalin thrilled him as it sunk in that he was free. The few shillings he had earned while inside was all the money he had but it would be enough to see him home to Maggie's place. He looked forward to some home-cooked food and to seeing his mother again; she seemed to be coping well and staying off the drink. He would get a job as a painter again without much trouble.

As he turned to walk to the nearby railway station, a familiar girl's voice took him by surprise.

'Hello, Harold.'

Another exhilarating adrenalin rush shot through him. It was Dora, of course, sitting on the bench outside the gate. The great pleasure he felt at the sight of her took him by surprise.

'G'day, Dora. What are you doing here?'

She smiled nervously, not sure what his reaction was going to be. She wondered if he understood that it wasn't her fault that she hadn't been able to visit him. 'I'm w–waiting for you, of course.'

'Jeez, it's good to see you. How've you been, good?'

His response, warm and congenial, melted her nervousness. She felt like smothering him with kisses but knew better than that, well aware that Harold was uncomfortable with public displays of affection; in fact, he abhorred them. They walked together, chatting away as they'd never done before. They reached the railway station but instead of getting on a train they kept walking, all the way back through South Brisbane, across the Victoria Bridge and into the city. He was surprised that Annie Milner had allowed her to meet him. He was further surprised to learn that Annie had invited him to have dinner with them that night. He'd been certain that she wouldn't want her daughter to maintain her relationship with a gaolbird. He declined. He just wanted to have a night at home.

They arrived at Maggie's place just before noon. Within minutes, he'd disposed of a large pile of sandwiches and numerous cups of tea. Dora and Maggie spent the afternoon gossiping. Harold, after his first wholesome food for months, suddenly felt exhausted and fell asleep on a cot on the front landing. He awoke the next morning, initially unsure of his whereabouts, then relieved and happy to realise he was free. After a breakfast of sausages and eggs on toast, he took a bath and then called around to see Irish, who lived in the next street. They collected Tommy and made their way to the Valley to pick up Jock and Dora. The boys were excited to hear about Harold's time in prison but he made it clear that he wasn't keen to talk about it and would rather forget it all as quickly as possible. They didn't raise the subject again.

That night, they all went to the Milners' house for dinner. Harold had never felt completely at ease with Annie. She was a hard-working professional housekeeper and laundress. Moderately good-looking, with long brown hair usually worn in a stern bun at the back, she was shortish and thickset. Annie was a confirmed atheist who'd never seen fit to marry, and her offspring represented the fruits of separate romantic dalliances. A true feminist, she'd never sought assistance from their fathers or the state for their support and was quite capable of – and happy – making her own way in a tough world. She possessed an acid and sarcastic turn of phrase and never hesitated to use it to take someone down a peg or two if she disliked them.

She could also be warm and charming when the mood took her, welcoming a select group of her children's friends to her small home each Sunday night for a meal, usually of cold cuts and salad followed by a feast of hot scones, strawberry jam and whipped cream. It was a weekly treat that she was happy to provide for them. To show their appreciation, Harold and his mates would often bring a small gift for Annie. Although she knew these gifts were probably not paid for with their hard-earned cash, she always made a tremendous fuss about their generosity.

A rousing, sometimes heated discussion of current affairs was regularly on the agenda after dinner, usually over a game of cards. Annie was extremely proud of her knowledge of the Australian political system, so she was particularly fond of Johnno Mann. Fortunately for the young man, their leanings were in a similar direction, decidedly leftist. Johnno was eager for the day, soon to come, when he'd be old enough to become a member of his beloved Labor Party and pursue a career in politics.

*

Clarrie was released from Boggo Road not long after Harold. The body of the gangster whose disappearance had been the motivating factor for his 'holiday' had been found and the authorities had declared his cause of death to be a 'fatal accident'. Clarrie had been informed by his contacts in the south that it was safe to return to Melbourne and he made a booking at the interstate railway station to travel home.

Towards the end of Harold's sentence, he and Clarrie had made an arrangement to meet at the Wickham for a drink when Clarrie was released. They were joined by Tommy, Jock, Irish and Geoff Davies, who had moved from Melbourne to Brisbane to live permanently. Geoff was a true character. Harold reckoned he was a 'mad bastard' but he loved his company. Geoff had gone close to becoming a member of the Victorian parliament the year previously. He'd long contended that most people didn't know, or care particularly, who they were voting for in state elections and that anyone could get elected if he wanted to. When challenged by a drinking mate that it couldn't be done, he decided to prove it could. So he changed his name by deed poll to Geoffrey Adams. His surname saw him placed at the top of the ballot form for his local seat and, with the aid of the donkey vote that he'd anticipated, he went within a couple of hundred votes of success.

It was a Friday night and the group settled into a session typical of the kind that took place in the many hundreds of pubs throughout Queensland, where hotels closed later than in the south. There was raucous yarning, lying, skiting and general discussion, debate and argument, mostly about politics and sport. In their group, Geoff held the floor for most of the evening. A gregarious and gifted raconteur, he regaled them and other groups of drinkers with tales, mostly fictitious, of famous American gangsters, many of whom he maintained that he'd met. His enthusiastic attention to detail, complete with gunshot and machine-gun sound effects, left all but the most cynical of his audience in no doubt as to their basis in fact. When Geoff Davies was around, everybody was thoroughly entertained.

It was only a matter of time until the drink began to take its effect on Harold's manner. His mates knew the signs well. His conversation began to become edgy and his disposition unpleasant, picky. His facial expression became unmistakably smug, arrogant. Trouble was brewing. Tommy and Jock made their usual well-advised quiet exit and urged Geoff to do the same, which he did, only too happily. He had a pretty young wife, Tess, and a tasty dinner to go home to anyway. Before long, Irish left as well. He was doing a bit of starting price bookmaking and needed to have a clear head for the following day's races. Clarrie remained with his young mate until closing time. He'd had plenty of experience in handling hotheads but had never dealt with any as persistent as this one. He managed, though, to expertly deflect every one of the young bloke's attempts to start something. He'd booked a room at the Shamrock, so after closing time, he was able to walk most of the way home with Harold and they arranged to meet in the bar there when the pub opened the following morning.

Ten a.m. and Clarrie, having eaten a large breakfast, made his way down to the bar. A bellyful of beer was going to help him sleep for at least part of the two-day train trip home that he was to start that afternoon. In walked Harold, grievously hung-over but nevertheless prepared to resume hostilities; he was shaky of hand and foggy of mind but surprisingly steady of foot.

'G'day, young Fingo,' Clarrie greeted him, rather more brightly than Harold considered decent at this time of the morning. 'You were a bit out of order last night, ya know. No wonder yer always in trouble with the coppers. Anyone else and I'd have sat ya on yer arse,' he joked.

'Just as well ya never tried,' shot back the young bloke, although he knew he'd probably be no match for the much larger man. 'I'd have punched holes in ya!'

Clarrie laughed out loud. This was the reason that he liked this young lair so much. Would he never take a backward step? He shook his head in mock exasperation. 'Jesus, you're a cheeky bastard!' He turned towards the barmaid who had been waiting patiently to take their order. 'Give this mug a beer, will ya, love, and one for me as well,' he said, and they chuckled together as they consumed the first of many satisfying ales for the day.

Clarrie left for the railway station at about three o'clock that afternoon, extending to Harold an invitation to come to Melbourne any time he liked and to look him up as soon as he got there. 'Just ask around the docks. Everyone knows where to find me' were his parting instructions to Harold, who by now was well on his way to another night of drunkenness and, if things followed their usual pattern, some kind of physical conflict.

15
Shortened Up!

By force, hath overcome but half his foe

John Milton (1608–74), 'Paradise Lost'

Time, as it will, exerted its powers of healing and with its passing, Harold found that his dreadful grief over the loss of Kitty was beginning to ease a little. He realised that he was confronting a new and different foe, however. He recognised that his weakness for the drink was developing into dependence and he would have to take measures to at least cut back.

He started drinking less and spending more time with Dora. Most Friday evenings he would take her to the dance at the Railway Institute Hall towards the top of Edward Street, in the city. He made the supreme effort to remain sober and never disappoint her, because dancing was her favourite pastime and gave her a chance to dress up in one of the frocks that she so expertly sewed for herself. She favoured pretty floral patterns and her dresses always suited her slim, shapely figure. She loved arriving at the dance with her handsome boyfriend and imagined that she was the envy of every girl present. Almost invariably, Jock and his girlfriend, Winifred, would accompany them. They would set off at around seven-thirty for the short walk to Brunswick Street station, where they caught the train to Central and the adjacent dance hall.

One sultry late-summer night, though, Winifred had taken ill with the flu and Jock, who hated dancing anyway, decided to stay at home. Harold and Dora made their way from Dora's place to the station, walking left along Ann Street and right along Barlow, where the Fortitude Valley post office stood, opposite Mr Wills's grocery shop. The post office was an impressive stone building with tiled entrances, in the style of most government buildings of the day, with the Australian coat of arms displayed proudly above the main entrance.

Dora could never understand why Harold felt so ill-at-ease when she tried to take his arm. As had become their habit, he walked half a pace or so in front of her and to the side, his hands in his pockets, contributing minimally in response to her efforts to make conversation. He walked briskly, seeming, as he did most of the time, to be lost in thought, existing in a world of his own. For some time Dora had been admiring a pair of shoes in the window of the clothing store opposite the post office and was saving up the money to buy them. She paused momentarily to admire them once more, oblivious to the fact that Harold had already crossed Ann Street. By the time she turned to follow him, he was nowhere to be seen.

As she arrived at the opposite street corner, her attention was jolted by the sound of a muffled shriek of pain. She was by now standing near one of the entrances to the post office. Peering into the recessed doorway in the semi-darkness, she was shocked at the sight of two hefty men bashing another man with batons. They had knocked him to the ground. Although he was valiantly attempting to defend himself and get back on his feet, it was clear he was hopelessly overpowered.

When she realised that it was Harold who was being attacked, she screamed impulsively. She looked desperately up and down the street for someone who might be able to assist them but in this part of the Valley it was always quiet at this time of night. Her scream, however, attracted the attention of one of the aggressors. He was Constable Muller and his accomplice was Knobby Clark. Neither policeman was in uniform – Clark in a suit, Muller in shirtsleeves.

Although gripped by panic and terror, Dora stepped forward and found her voice. 'Stop it, stop it, leave him alone!' she cried. Muller took her roughly by the arm. 'Shut up, you,' he ordered.

Harold was prone and clearly in agony. Clark drew his revolver and smashed the side of Harold's head with it. Harold struggled to maintain consciousness, certain that if he lost it, he'd lose his life as well. Blood gushed from his left temple and his ear but he remained alert enough to hear the police sergeant's words: 'I hate you, Fingleton, you rotten, criminal bastard. I'd love to blow your fuckin' head off.'

'You wouldn't have the fuckin' guts,' Harold spat back.

Dora was horrified. Her mind raced. Somewhere within she could hear herself screaming, 'Harold, oh Harold, please shut up. Don't be so stupid' – but no words escaped her lips. His audacity sent a surge of anger through the copper. He grabbed Harold's throat with his massive left hand as with his right he cocked the pistol's hammer.

'Oh, wouldn't I?'

'Jesus, Knobby,' shouted an alarmed Muller, 'don't do it, don't do it! This piece of shit isn't worth it!' It was good advice. It was also self-interested. He didn't fancy being buckled as an accomplice to murder. By now, Dora, still held firmly in Muller's grasp, was almost faint with sheer terror.

Clark regained his self-control and slowly released his grip. Standing upright, he allowed himself the pleasure of one more kick to Harold's ribs. It landed with a gruesome thud, causing the young man to gasp in pain. Holstering his pistol, Clark straightened his jacket and, with a shrug, indicated to Muller that it was time to get going. Brushing past Dora, he momentarily set his eyes firmly on hers. 'One word from you to anyone about any of this, you little slut, and you'll get some of the same.'

Dora was seriously offended by the unfair slur on her character but reacted with a series of swift, jittery nods. The policeman knew that she'd gotten his message. He would have absolutely nothing to fear from her.

As if to test his luck to the absolute limits, Harold called after the sergeant as he stepped out onto the footpath: 'I told ya you wouldn't have the guts, Clark, ya fuckin' animal.' Clark halted, momentarily tempted to return and finish the job but Muller, asserting more authority than he had ever before, grabbed his superior in a bear hug and managed to hustle him away. Harold's insult was noted, however, for future reference.

Dora kneeled beside him, unsure of what to do next. She removed her handkerchief from her purse and dabbed at the blood that was flowing freely down Harold's face – from his nose and mouth now, as well as the side of his head. The tiny piece of cotton cloth was virtually useless, so she used the skirt of her dress to wipe away as much of the gore as she could. She realised that she wasn't achieving much. 'Harold, will you be all right here while I go and get Jock and Mum?' she asked. 'I'll only be a few minutes.'

'No, no, don't get 'em, I'll be right,' said Harold, attempting to raise himself up on one elbow. He couldn't and slumped back to the ground with a heavy, slow groan. 'On second thought, maybe you'd better,' he murmured.

'I'll be as quick as I can, Harold.'

'Good, Dora, I'll wait here.' As he mumbled the words, he realised how absurd they sounded. He didn't think he'd be able to go anywhere even if the building burned down.

Within minutes, Dora arrived back at the scene with her mother and brother. Annie's strength surprised him, as did her gentleness and sympathy as she and Jock lifted him to his feet. With them on either side supporting him, Harold stumbled, and was part-carried, part-dragged back to number 12 Patrick Street and at least temporary safety.

Annie bathed and dressed his wounds and wrapped his ribs tightly. Jock gave up his bed to his mate and set up one to use for the time being on the living-room couch. Harold settled down for an uncomfortable night. He wouldn't sleep, not only because of the physical pain but also the mental turmoil stirred up by his hatred for his assailants. As Dora said good night and left him to his private anguish, hoping that he might get some rest, he muttered: 'I'm gunna kill that mongrel bastard one day.'

'Please don't talk like that, Harold, that's just being silly,' admonished Dora. His statement did not sound like idle bravado and she feared for the future, sensing the depth of the enmity that it contained.

16

A Little Discretion

Travel is glamorous only in retrospect

Paul Theroux (1941–)

Annie assured Harold that he was welcome to stay with them for a while, until he felt well enough to look after himself, at least. She was smart enough to know that he wouldn't be safe anywhere else, not with Clark in his current frame of mind. He took advantage of the invitation. Maggie and Nellie would visit him and bring him treats such as home-made scones and pikelets. Dora spent every spare moment with her patient and in the evenings rushed home from her job at a shirt manufacturers in Ann Street, in the city, excited that she had the opportunity to look after him and spoil him a little. She was an expert machinist, entrusted, along with only two others on the factory staff, to sew tailor-made shirts from start to finish, rather than undertake the piecework that most of the others did.

Harold was beginning to feel a twinge of uneasiness. He hadn't been treated with such kindness in his life. He spent most of his time in recovery thinking of Dora and found himself counting the hours until she returned home. Emotions such as these were foreign to him. He was edgy about where they might lead. Perhaps it was time to back off.

He, Jock and the others discussed whether it was wiser for him to get away from Brisbane for a while. They would miss their mate but couldn't see the sense in Harold hanging around – it was well within Clark's capability and authority to make life even more complicated for him. The events of that Friday night were evidence enough that he meant to show no mercy. Although it annoyed him to admit it, Harold knew that what they said was true. He wouldn't be safe no matter where he went in Brisbane and neither would anyone who was with him, including Dora. He had to face the fact that some discretion was advisable right now. It had nothing to do with giving in to Clark or letting him win. He would love nothing more than a one-on-one fair go with the copper but that wasn't likely to happen. Clark's resources were insurmountable. The smart thing to do was to find some breathing space – but where?

Harold recalled Clarrie's parting words about coming to

Melbourne whenever he felt like it. He mentioned it to his mates.

Jock piped up, 'I met a bloke at the races by the name of Jimmy Blunt who works for a horse trainer down at Doomben Racecourse. Jim was a jockey but he was useless, never rode a winner. All the dieting to control his weight got 'im down so he gave it away. Anyway, now he's the strapper for a real good horse that they're taking south for the big autumn races. The owner's paying for 'im to go with it to look after it properly. They're going by rail. Jimmy's a good bloke. I reckon you could travel with 'im if you wanted to. There wouldn't be any conductors checking for tickets in a freight carriage. I'll take you down to meet 'im if you like – see what he thinks.'

Harold thought for a moment. He didn't need to travel with anybody. He could just as easily jump a train and go on his own but if Jock's mate Jimmy seemed like a good bloke it might be nice to have some company for what would be at least a three-day trip, with stops for loading and unloading freight. The following Saturday, Jock introduced him to Blunt. He and Harold took a liking to each other immediately and Jim fancied the idea of having a travelling companion, so they made their arrangements.

If one was marginally athletic, it wasn't very difficult to board a slowly accelerating freight train; not long after it had departed the goods yard in the dusk one late February afternoon, Harold, with Jim's assistance, had become a stowaway. Having congratulated themselves on how easily it all went, the two young men settled in for the journey.

Despite the ever-present pungent smell of animal urine and excrement, the trip proved reasonably comfortable. There was no shortage of tobacco to smoke – Jim was flush with funds as a result of a good trot at the track of late and didn't mind sharing it with his travelling companion. There was also plenty of hay to rest on and no shortage of clean water to drink, kept on hand for the horse. Jimmy was engaging and amusing company, with numerous tales to tell of racing rorts and misadventures that helped to keep Harold's mind off the sad farewell that he'd shared with his mates and, especially, Dora. He'd left her in a state of utter despair – he was going far away and she was certain that she'd never see the boy she loved again.

He jumped off the train prior to its reaching the last station. Jimmy asked him to stay in touch – he might be able to tip him a winner at the races. But Harold had not the slightest interest in betting on horses or anything else. Gambling was one vice that held no attraction for him whatsoever. If ever he went to the races, it was for more nefarious pursuits. Having thanked his new pal for his hospitality, he set about finding his way to the Melbourne dockyards, where he hoped to get in touch with Clarrie Weston.

Any stranger asking questions at the docks was eyed with

suspicion and Harold found his inquiries either ignored or met with a 'Sorry, mate, don't know 'im.'

Within a short time, however, Clarrie had found him instead. He welcomed his young friend warmly. 'G'day, son. Good to see you. What're you doin' down here?'

'I thought I'd give it a try. Things were gettin' real warm back home. That copper bastard Clark – I told you about 'im before – he wants to kill me. I'm not scared of the mongrel but I didn't want any of me mates coppin' it on my account.' He didn't mention his concern for his girlfriend. 'Can you do anything about a job for me?'

'Yeah, I reckon so. I'll get you a start here if you like.'

'I wouldn't have a clue what I was doin'. How long would it take me to learn the ropes?'

'Don't let that worry you' was Clarrie's smirking reply. 'Just turn up on time every day 'n' come 'n' see me. Where are you stayin'?'

'I haven't got a place yet. I came straight here to see you.'

'Jesus, you stink! How did you travel down – in the back of a fuckin' garbage truck?'

Harold laughed and then explained about his mate's mate and stowing away in the stock carriage of the train.

'Well, you can stay at my place. My missus is a good sort; she'll be happy to meet you. I've told her about you. I'll be knockin' off in a few minutes. You can come home with me and have a bath. Are you hungry?'

'No, I'm right, me mate had money for food.' It wasn't entirely true. Harold hadn't eaten at all that day and it was now three-thirty in the afternoon but he didn't want to be too much of a nuisance. As it happened, a meal bigger than any he had ever seen was waiting for them when they arrived at Clarrie's place. A warm bath, big meal, comfortable mattress and a feeling of complete security ensured him a long and restful night's sleep.

Clarrie followed through on his offer and Harold started his new job two days later. As Clarrie had promised him, it was only a matter of turning up each day. There wasn't a lot to learn about his new profession, which involved, principally, cleaning and repainting the inside of ships' hulls to protect them from rust. It wasn't particularly difficult work but it was time-consuming and very well paid.

The dockers were disinclined to overtax themselves and a lot of Harold's time seemed to be spent playing cards. Morning and afternoon smokos and lunch breaks seemed to have no strict time parameters. It didn't really suit him – he'd rather have been busy doing something constructive – but his new workmates were a friendly lot once he'd won their trust, and he was eager to learn about the games they played, especially their favourite, five hundred.

He was well received by the dockers for the fact that, unlike a lot of other young blokes, he didn't seem to need to try to impress anyone. There was an evident self-assurance about his manner. He deported himself with a disaffectedly cocky, confident air – upright of stature, shoulders defiantly back – but he wasn't given to boasting, or in fact talking at all, about the things he'd done and seen. Such an attitude was welcome in a workplace like this one. Most of the men had private issues that they preferred to keep to themselves. It wasn't in their nature to discuss their problems or their business with others. There were plenty of other things to talk about. The hospital casualty wards beckoned anyone who became too nosey.

Harold stayed with the Westons for a fortnight. With the pay for his first couple of weeks' work, he was then able to rent a bedsitter in South Melbourne.

He had decided that he'd best keep his nose clean in the Victorian capital. Because he trusted Clarrie and appreciated his hospitality, he felt it would be bad form to get into any strife. That meant he'd need to stay off the drink. His workmates would enjoy a few beers at the pub after work each afternoon before going home but he'd have soft drink. It surprised and impressed Clarrie because he'd seen Harold at his worst. The rest of the men respected him for it as well.

He enjoyed their company but it irked him that most of their conversations at the pub seemed to revolve around one thing only and that was Australian Rules football, about which he knew absolutely nothing. The sport was a virtual nonentity in his home city and he'd never seen it played.

Any attempt to discuss or explain the finer points of the game of Rugby League with any of them was met with blank stares and scant interest. Recognising that the players must be great athletes and that their supporters shared the same kind of devotion he had to his own sporting heroes, he resolved that once the football season started he would go to a few Rules matches to see what all the fuss was about.

As soon as Clarrie left the pub, so too would he.

Clarrie provided enough odd jobs to keep Harold busy on weekends as well. The illegal gambling and sly-grog entrepreneurs about the town kept the police quiet by giving them protection payments. Clarrie had set himself up as a go-between, collecting and passing on payments and receiving a percentage of the graft money. He had a number of men helping out with the operation, which had to be performed with the utmost circumspection, of course. As he knew how to keep his mouth shut, Harold was well suited to the job. The extra money the work provided enabled him to buy some much-needed warm clothes and make his previously unfurnished digs comfortable. The place had a wood-burning stove and all he really needed was a bed, an icebox and a table and chair. He also bought some cricket gear because he'd decided that he wouldn't mind a game of cricket if he could get one. After attending training with one of the local clubs, he was selected to play for a minor team for the brief remainder of the 1928 cricket season.

A Little Discretion

He had turned nineteen and autumn had begun to blow in. Up until then he had dealt with the summer heat easily enough. It was the cold and the wind that he hated. He had little in the way of body fat to keep him warm and as the weather grew chillier, so too did his disposition and his opinion of the great city of Melbourne. Autumn would degenerate into winter in a month or two and he was rapidly growing tired of the constant drizzling rain and the occasional bitter winds that scythed in from the Antarctic, threatening to freeze his very core. He decided that it might be best if he headed for warmer climes. Clarrie was disappointed to see him go but gave the youngster his assurance that there would always be a job for him should he wish to return.

17

The Country Life

Anybody can be good in the country

Oscar Wilde (1854–1900)
The Picture of Dorian Gray

The new Federal Parliament House, a splendid, rambling triple-storeyed building, had been officially opened almost a year before Harold arrived in Canberra. His trek north had taken him nearly two weeks because when he'd set out, he was in no hurry and he'd decided to see what rural Victoria had to offer. He'd hitched rides where he could and had walked many miles, often sleeping rough, on his journey.

Many of the tradesmen and labourers who'd spent the past dozen or so years on the construction site were only too happy to move on, some to return to their country homes; others, bored with country life and flush with funds saved from their generous salaries, headed for the larger towns and cities.

Extra painters were desperately needed to maintain the building, inside and out, so, in order to preserve his meagre cash stores, he decided to apply for a job. Although he hadn't been granted his master painter's certificate and was still qualified only as an apprentice, his services were eagerly taken up. He was soon plying his trade, so competently it turned out, that he quickly became a member of the full-time maintenance crews that would keep the new building up to the standard necessary for one of such pre-eminence.

He now had a job for as long as he wanted it, had taken a room in a hotel in Queanbeyan, a bus ride away from work, and life was good, except that the weather in the area was harshly cold at times. Caps, scarves, gloves and an overcoat, items that he'd never needed in his home city, became his normal apparel.

There was a Rugby League football club based at Queanbeyan and it was part of a viable and progressive New South Wales rural competition. He was selected in the first-grade team immediately after turning out for one training session – to play in his preferred position at centre three-quarter. The club's football training system was not overly taxing or time-consuming. In the late afternoon on Tuesdays and Thursdays the players would gather at the training field for a workout that would take roughly one hour to complete.

A few laps of the oval to warm up, a talk about match tactics from the coach, followed by a game of touch football was the normal, simple routine and then it was off to the nearest pub to slake their thirsts and undo most of the good work, inconsiderable though it may have been.

Competition matches usually took place on Sundays. Every second Sunday, clubs would host a visiting team – the next week they would travel by train or bus, depending on the distance to be traversed, to their opponent's home ground. Games were followed by a social evening at the home team's clubhouse, if they had one, or more often at a local hall. How civilised these functions were varied with the outcome of the match. Referees, often members of the local police, were provided by the home side. If the visiting team lost, they often believed that the cause was the unfairness of the refs. The situation could get pretty hostile and those hostilities – temporarily halted at the end of the game by the traditional shaking of hands – were often raucously resumed a few hours later under the influence of drink. It was not unusual for some members of the visiting team to arrive back at their home town a day or so later than expected, after an appearance in court. In the interests of inter-town harmony, charges were more often than not dropped. Most men made it home for Tuesday night training.

Some of the more talented players undertook to do extra training on their own or in small groups. Harold was one of these. He set out to train harder than his opponents. His reflexes sharpened and his strength and fitness developed. He was maturing into his prime. Despite having a habit of harsh self-criticism, he realised that he was playing brilliant football, his optimal level of fitness now backing up his tremendous natural ability and courage. He was feared by opponents for his timing and frightening aggression in tackles and his evasive ability, well honed in the back streets of Brisbane as a kid. He could, as he termed it, 'put a bloke on his left or right foot' and sidestep him at will. His opponent would be left in his wake, bewildered and empty-handed.

Word reached him that he was being considered for inclusion in a team to represent New South Wales Combined Country. The team would take part in a selection trial for the New South Wales side that would play against Queensland in the annual interstate series. The newly appointed Australian and Queensland captain, Tommy Gorman, had played against Harold when his job had transferred him to Canberra for a time. Gorman had recommended him to the national selectors as a player of the highest quality. Possible international stardom beckoned, depending upon how he performed on the field.

Fate would have none of it. In a moment of carelessness at work, Harold fell from a trestle and smashed his right ankle.

If he'd managed the injury properly during his rehabilitation, he may have returned to top-level football, but he ignored medical advice. Early in the piece, he discarded the uncomfortable and restrictive cast that he should have worn for the next few months. His ankle never fully healed, was weak and was subject to spraining regularly from then onwards. No longer as speedy and elusive on the field, he lost some of his edge. Adversaries who had been no match for him before were now his equals.

His confidence and his dreams shattered, the frustration and anger that he'd lately managed to overcome returned. Sobriety was no longer of any advantage to him and he could see no reason to deny his compulsive alcoholic urges. Constant drunkenness and brawling soon earned him expulsion from the Queanbeyan club and, eventually, the sack from his job as well.

Having spent the best part of two years there, Harold left the Canberra area and decided to live for a while in Goulburn, further along the Hume Highway towards Sydney. There he took a room at one of the hotels in the town. He didn't bother to find a job and it wasn't long before his money ran out.

It would have been time to move on, had it not been for the fact that he had a six-month sentence to serve in Goulburn prison for assault and battery. For once, he had not been the aggressor: someone had king-hit him for no apparent reason. He retaliated by giving his attacker a thrashing that resulted in hospitalisation. But he was beginning to wonder if it might be a better idea to lose a fight, because as the victor you were more likely to find yourself in trouble with the law.

Goulburn had a well-earned reputation for being the toughest prison in the state. If one was unlucky enough to be incarcerated there during the normally freezing winter, as Harold was, it was doubly harsh. He had the added pleasure of spending a week in solitary confinement because he was silly enough – and cheeky enough – to offer to 'pay extra' for another blanket. By the time he was released, he'd become more morose and desperately miserable than he'd ever been.

18
Ravished

*Son, you'll never know real pain until
you think you're gonna starve to death*

Harold William Fingleton (1909–86)

His term in Goulburn served, within weeks Harold was officially a vagrant. The few shillings that he'd had in his pocket were gone and work was seemingly impossible to find. He read in a discarded newspaper about the onset of a worldwide depression following the collapse of the stock market in faraway New York. Like most Australians, he was yet to understand what it all meant but the country was already beginning to feel the full, disastrous ramifications of it.

He was determined about one thing: he'd served his last stint behind prison walls. No matter what the circumstances, he wouldn't take any risk that might lead to another gaol term, he promised himself. He was aware that his biggest problem was his alcoholism, because when he drank he lost his self-control. That wasn't much of a problem at the moment, however – he had no money to buy grog. He didn't want to pilfer money to survive, because that had the potential to land him back in hot water and a cold cell again.

He went from door to door of private homes and businesses, big and small, in Goulburn, offering his services for any kind of work that might be available. It had been weeks since he'd eaten anything substantial, just the odd piece of fruit or leftover scraps that he could cadge from a kind shopkeeper or passer-by. He'd quickly learned that it was a waste of time to ask anyone for money. Anyway, theft and burglary had become so rampant that people carried as little cash as possible and kept almost none in their homes.

He was feeling sicker by the day. The searing headache and cramping pains in his stomach and his muscles were becoming worse, to the point where he was beginning to wonder how sick he'd have to feel before he starved to death.

After a day of door knocking, he squatted with his back against the wall of a hotel, his arms folded around his skinny legs, his head resting on his knees. He'd just been inside asking the owner for work and had been refused yet again – not with animosity – there simply wasn't anything for him. Harold felt more comfortable in this hunched pose.

Somehow, it seemed to make the pain and dizziness subside a little. When he felt stronger, he'd head to Sydney and see Mollie and Lucy. He'd be welcome there for a while at least, he assured himself.

A hand came to rest upon his shoulder. He lifted his head and as his blurred vision sharpened, he found himself looking at a slim, well-dressed man. His hair was silver and slick, beneath a black homburg, his face pale. He carried a cane with a metal handle in his gloved hand.

'Finding the going a bit tough, are you, son?' The man's voice was cultured, deep and resonant – surprising to Harold, considering the stranger's slight build.

'Yeah, I s'pose you could say that,' he replied dismissively. His voice was little more than a husky whisper. He was loath to engage in conversation with strangers at any time, but in his present condition, it was a real effort to do so. He resumed his original pose, hoping that the fellow would go away and leave him alone.

'I might be able to give you a bit of a hand. Would you like that?'

He lifted his head again: 'Just give me some work or some food if you can, mate. That's all I want.'

'I think we can manage that. Why don't you come with me and we'll see if we can't help you to feel a bit better, eh?'

'Come where?' Harold knew instinctively that there had to be a catch to all of this.

The man beckoned a driver dressed in a grey suit and cap, who had been standing at the open rear door of the man's highly polished black car. 'Back to my house. There's plenty of food and drink there, and a warm bath and a comfortable bed. You'd like that, would you not?'

'Yeah, of course I would. What do I have to do for it?'

'Why don't we discuss that on the way home?'

Harold shrugged his shoulders and hesitated momentarily, before rising to his feet. As he did so, he swooned, dizziness all but overcoming him. With the assistance of the driver, the well-dressed man helped Harold into the back seat of the car and got in beside him. Night was about to fall as the chauffeur turned over the engine and drove onto the Hume Highway. Harold had no idea in which direction they were travelling but hoped it wouldn't be a long journey. He knew only that he must have something to eat – and soon.

'We'll be home in about an hour. What's your name, son?'

'Harold.'

'Where do you come from, Harold?'

'Brisbane originally, mate, but I've been on the track for a while.'

Their journey continued for some minutes without further conversation. The drone of the engine and the warmth and comfort of the vehicle lulled Harold into a semiconscious, drowsy state. He felt tired and weak.

The man broke the silence. 'You're a good-looking young man. How did you find yourself in this position?'

Harold was no better at small talk now than he'd ever been and was uninterested in telling this complete stranger his life story. 'Look, mate, I know you're not doing me any favours for nothin'. I'm starvin' and all I want is somethin' to eat. What do you want from me?'

'Ah, a young chap who speaks his mind! Good! You've clearly been around the place and understand how things work. In that case . . .' He took Harold's left hand and placed it in his lap. He proceeded to undo the buttons of his trousers.

'Not on your fuckin' life, mate,' Harold responded sharply. He rapidly withdrew his hand from the man's lap and automatically and instantaneously formed a fist.

'Are you sure, son? There's plenty of nice food waiting for you at my place and you might not eat again for a long time yet, if at all. Surely you don't want to die of starvation.'

'You can stick your food up your arse. I'm no fuckin' poofter.'

'All right, then, if that's the way you feel … William, pull the car over, will you, and let Harold out.'

'You're not gunna let me out here in the middle of nowhere, are you?'

'You leave me no alternative, Harold. I'm not interested in wasting my time on you. You must know that everything has its price.'

The vehicle stopped at the side of the highway. Harold got out but as he did, he felt the sharp stab of a massive hunger pang. He turned as if to slam the door, but swooned and, after reeling briefly, fainted where he stood.

*

When he awoke, he was lying, fully clothed, on a comfortable double bed. He felt terribly weak. His stomach still ached with hunger. The bedspread and the pillows smelt fresh and clean. There was a fire in the corner of the room that gave the place a pleasant flickering light. He reckoned it must've been early evening. As he sat up on the side of the bed, his head swam. Deciding to explore the place to see if he could find some food, he stood on trembling legs, exited the room and shambled his way down a staircase to the ground-floor foyer of what appeared to be a large sandstone country house. He entered a room to his left. It was lit by candelabra.

'Welcome back to the land of the living, young man.'

He turned to see the man who had picked him up the previous evening, sitting in an armchair, a glass of what Harold assumed was alcohol in hand. He was clothed in a full-length silk dressing gown and slippers and was wearing a cravat.

'I'm just about to have my supper. You'd like something to eat, wouldn't you?'

'Of course I would. Where am I?' His voice was even huskier than it had been before. He tried to clear his throat and failed. 'The last thing I can remember is gettin' out of your car.'

'Yes, but you fainted as you did so and I didn't have the heart to leave you there. We might have lost you. We couldn't allow that to happen, could we?'

Harold gave a shrug but didn't answer. The man stood and beckoned him to follow. They entered the adjacent dining room, where two places had been set, one at each side of a large oval-shaped dining table. A servant brought in two bowls of freshly cooked chicken broth. Harold was invited to sit but needed no such invitation. He drank the soup straight from the bowl and disposed of the bread roll that rested on a small plate to one side. His hunger only partially satisfied, he asked if he could have more.

'Certainly you may,' the man replied and rang a tiny bell that sat before him on the table. In a moment, the servant reappeared. 'Bring our guest some more broth, please, and serve the main course in a few minutes.'

Attempts at conversation by his host were met with mainly grunts as Harold greedily attacked his first real meal in months. By the time he'd eaten his second helping of dessert and consumed his third glass of beer, he was feeling bloated and a little queasy. He'd been able to learn a bit about his host, who told him that he was a single, retired doctor and that his family had lived in the district for four generations. He said that he'd given Harold a sedative injection the night before to ensure that he would sleep well and regain some of his strength.

Harold sat back in his chair and looked around him. The dining room was the fanciest he'd ever seen, not that he'd seen many fancy dining rooms. From the paintings and opulent furnishings it was clear his host was a very wealthy man. He realised that the topic of what had happened in the car the previous evening would soon, of necessity, be broached. A brief, awkward silence was broken by the good doctor.

'Now, young fellow, it seems from your conduct last night that you took offence to my approach towards you. Do you still feel the same way?'

'Of course,' was Harold's terse reply. He resisted the impulse to elaborate.

'Well, how do you expect to repay me for my kindnesses?'

'I didn't ask for any of this,' Harold retorted. 'But if you want payment, I'll do any work about the place that you want to give me, for as long as it takes.'

'Commendable attitude, indeed,' conceded his host, 'but I'm afraid that that won't do. No, that won't do at all. I don't suppose you'd like to reconsider?'

As the man spoke, Harold began to feel a tingling in his fingers and light-headedness. Suddenly, he was having trouble forming his words and was beginning to see stars before his eyes. He hesitated to think that he may have been slipped a drug of some kind but time seemed to slow down and his arms and legs gradually became heavier. He couldn't believe it. He'd seen this kind of thing on the silver screen but it didn't happen to people in real life, did it?

He did not lose consciousness entirely but he was unable to muster the strength or coordination to mount a defence against the rape to which he was repeatedly subjected during the following hours, by both the doctor and his chauffeur. He simply had no power in his limbs whatsoever. With the drug in his system, he could feel no physical pain from their debauchery but the indignity of it wrenched at his mind, until eventually he collapsed from sheer mental exhaustion and passed out.

*

The following morning, after they'd finished with him, he was bundled into the boot of the car, still in a very weak, drug-induced haze. After a journey that seemed to last for hours, he was dumped at the roadside. They'd at least clothed him. Eventually, he regained full awareness. He was consumed with rage. He had to find his captors and exact his revenge. But he had absolutely no idea where to find them or the house, had no clue even as to which direction he should head or where the road that he was on might take him.

He began to walk and suddenly felt the pain of the bruising in his rectum. The full impact of what had happened hit him. A dark, swarming cloud enveloped his mind. He dropped to his knees and curled up into a ball of gut-wrenched anger. He sobbed for a few moments and then emitted a scream that rolled across the adjacent flatland.

'Fuck – fuck it. Fuck everything and every-fuckin'-body!' he bellowed through clenched teeth. 'When's a man gunna get a fuckin' break!' He sobbed deeply for some time and then, realising the futility of self-pity, managed to calm himself down. Within moments, a long-forgotten impulse resurfaced. He began to blame himself for everything that had happened. Had he managed his life better, this wouldn't have befallen him. It was all his own fault and he'd gotten what he deserved …

He began to walk again, his mind engaged in a battle with itself as he tried to work out why he felt that it was his fault. He walked and walked, his body strengthened by the large meal he'd eaten the night before. In a while, guilt gave way again to the pressing determination to make his attackers pay for what they'd done to him. He felt relieved in a way: he'd hated the way his guilt had made him feel.

A couple of hours or so along the track, he came to a T-junction. He wondered for a moment which way he should turn. Unsure where either direction might take him, he decided to sit down, rest and wait. After a while, he was able to hitch a ride with a farmer who was on his way, in his rattling farm truck, to the Sydney markets with some produce. He asked the man if he was travelling via Goulburn. If he could get back there, someone might be able to give him some information about the blokes who'd raped him and then he could get square.

'We're a long, long way from Goulburn, son,' the farmer told him. 'It'd take you half the day to git back there.'

'Do you know of any quacks that live near here?'

The farmer shook his head. He lived forty miles away and didn't know the area.

Harold realised that for the time being he had little choice but to shelve his plans for retribution. As this bloke was headed for the big city, he might as well stick with him. He could look up Mollie there.

19

The Big Smoke

City life. Millions of people being lonesome together

Henry David Thoreau (1817–62)

Harold gently rapped on the door of the terrace house in Cascade Street, Paddington. It was early morning and he hoped his sister would not yet have left for the day.

'I'll get it, Mollie – I wonder who can be calling at this hour.' Rapid slippered footsteps shuffled along a linoleum-covered hallway. Lucy, still clad in her dressing gown, opened the door. 'Oh, dear Jesus ... Mollie, Mollie, it's Harold, it's Harold!' she screamed.

She threw her arms around the young man's neck as Mollie, already dressed for work, rushed – all but tumbled – down the steps that led from the second-storey bedrooms. She joined Lucy in the kissing and hugging, all noise and relief at the sight of him. She hadn't heard from him for months. He'd written to Dora occasionally but had instructed her not, under any circumstances, to supply his sister with the details of his travails.

The combined weight of their welcome was overpowering for him in his weakened state and he half-staggered through the door.

'My God, look at you; you're nothing but skin and bone. Are you all right, my darling?'

'Yeah, yeah, I'm okay,' he lied, his voice still husky with hunger and exhaustion. It had been a long, uncomfortable trip in the farmer's truck and he'd spent the night in a park somewhere in Newtown. He'd asked someone for directions to Paddington and had trudged the remainder of the way on foot.

'I'll get you something to eat – oh, Mollie, isn't it wonderful to see him?' Lucy said, releasing her grip on him and scurrying into the kitchen at the rear of the house.

Within minutes, Harold was having his fill of toast, tea, more toast, then poached eggs, bacon and more tea, all the while fielding, as evasively and convincingly as possible, question after question about where he'd been, what he'd been doing, did he have a job, had he heard from Dora recently, had he written to their mother – wasn't it good that she had stayed off the drink and was well – and seemingly dozens of other issues.

The entire welcoming process took its toll.

'Is there somewhere a man could have a sleep, please, Moll?' Harold asked. 'I'm fu – um . . . out on me feet.'

'Certainly, darling,' gushed his sister. 'Would you like to have a bath first? There's a blade razor in the bathroom if you want to shave as well. And the toilet's along the pathway out the back.'

It dawned on him that he certainly needed cleaning up. He would have preferred to let it go until he'd had some rest but, as he'd almost always done, he deferred to Mollie's polite recommendation. He felt a little uncomfortable with all the fuss they were making over him but at the same time he was enjoying the opportunity to completely relax in a spotlessly clean, secure environment – something he hadn't experienced for a long time.

'Do you have any luggage, dear?' Mollie asked.

'Nah, travellin' pretty light, Moll,' her brother replied.

He didn't have to say any more. Mollie was a wise, observant woman. Even as a child, her youngest brother had been fussy about his appearance. Now his clothes were dirty and worn and he looked tired, sad and world-weary. He'd always been a finicky eater. Now he scoffed down his food. There was a discernible droop to his normally square shoulders and he bore the downcast look of a defeated, much older man. He was very different from the cocky, strutting youth she remembered him to be. She dared not think what he must have been through to cause such changes. The best she could do was to gently care for him and trust that in time he'd reclaim the spirit now so conspicuously absent.

He slept soundly in the smallest of the three bedrooms, on the lower floor at the front, in one of his sister's nightdresses – comfortable, clean and well fed. He thought nothing of the fact that Mollie and Lucy would share the double bed in the main bedroom, sure that it was merely in order to make room for him. The remaining bedroom, he was to discover, doubled as a sewing room. He still, for all of his hard-earned wisdom, had no comprehension of the real nature of their relationship, the deep love that they shared.

*

Their voices, though hushed, roused him from his slumber. The room was in semi-darkness. He figured that he'd slept for the entire day. He reached for the oil lamp that had been shedding comforting, gentle light from the bedside table and turned it up to full strength.

Some new clothes, shoes, socks, underwear, pyjamas, slippers and a dressing gown had been placed on a trunk near the foot of the bed. His old clothes were nowhere to be seen. He donned the dressing gown and slippers, scrutinised his appearance in the full-length wardrobe mirror, ran his fingers through his hair and, deciding that he looked pretty good, opened the door to the narrow hall leading to the small living room.

Mollie and Lucy were preparing to leave for another day's work. He'd in fact slept through the day and for the entire night as well. He thanked them for his new clothes and was told to think nothing of their generosity.

'You'll be hungry again, you poor boy,' said Lucy and she scuttled, in her bustling fashion, into the kitchen to prepare some more food for him while he went to the outhouse.

He was eating his breakfast when they left, Lucy for the Royal Women's Hospital and Mollie to her job with Greenfield's, a Jewish clothing manufacturer in Surry Hills, the centre of the fashion trade in Sydney. Each of their workplaces was within easy walking distance of their comfortable rented home.

Before she left, Mollie asked if he had any money, knowing full well that he didn't. The pockets of his clothing had contained none. Although he said he did have money, she insisted that he take a few shillings to use if he wanted to go out during the day. They would see him for dinner that night. Mollie promised that Lucy would prepare him something he liked. Lucy was the willing designated cook for the pair, Mollie never having mastered the art. Mollie assured him that he was welcome to stay with them for as long as he needed to.

Despite their hospitality, Harold had no intention of becoming a burden to his sister and her friend. He thought it would be best if he found a job and a flat of his own in which to live, preferably close by. He'd heard that Sydney was a huge, fast-paced, sophisticated place, unlike his home city. It was somewhere he could fade into insignificance if he wished to, somewhere he could live in peace and quiet for a while. Because he was smart enough to stay out of trouble when he was sober and alert, he decided he would try to stay off the drink. He thought constantly of Dora and planned to ask her to join him when he had established himself.

He set about implementing his plan immediately, catching a tram in nearby Oxford Street to town. There he found his way to the general post office in Martin Place and sent a telegram to Clarrie to see if he had any contacts in Sydney who might be able to give him a job.

Sure enough, Clarrie wired him a reply, which was delivered to him at Mollie's place not long after he'd returned home. In it, Clarrie instructed him to take the telegram to a mate of his, Ronnie Hall, who was running a two-up school called Thommo's. The next night, Harold was working as a doorman at the game's premises, currently in Woolloomooloo.

The game was a 'floater'. Even though the proprietor paid generous amounts of graft money to the police, in order to keep up appearances he was required to shift from one location to another on a fairly regular basis, making it seem that the game was difficult for the police to locate and close down. Harold's job was to assist the head doorman, a tough bloke named Don Davis, in keeping order in the place. It was a sinecure because there was rarely any trouble. Losing or intoxicated gamblers were ill-advised to cause a commotion. The rare few who did were usually young, innocent novices ignorant of the protocols of illegal gambling dens and the dangers of misbehaving within their confines. They committed such an error only once if they were even half smart.

Life had become simple and easy again for Harold. Turn up for work at about eight p.m., be home by three or four in the morning at the latest, sleep until mid-morning and have the rest of the day to himself. He would go to a gymnasium for some training, play some snooker or pool, or go to a cinema or a football or cricket match. A ferry ride on the harbour was one of his favourite time wasters.

Within a couple of months, he'd surprised Mollie with his recovery. Young, resilient and happy in his job, he seemed to have regained his confidence. He was able to take a flat in Darlinghurst and buy some furniture. Pretty soon, he would be able to send for Dora, provided that she wished to come. He was pretty sure she would, judging by the tone of her regular letters.

Then he met Cathy. Catherine Churchill. The most perfect woman he'd ever seen. Here was a vision in grace and style, with ample flowing black hair that framed a beautiful face, a face that to Harold, bore the look of angels. Always impeccably and expensively dressed, with a slim, sensuous figure, she was older than he, in her mid-twenties, but his worldliness and flirtatious charm bridged the gap in their ages. They met at a café in Oxford Street one Saturday morning and were immediately infatuated with each other. They were soon lovers. They found a flat in Potts Point and moved in together.

Cathy had moved to the big city from her parents' home in Wollongong, south of Sydney, three years earlier. Since then, she said, she'd worked part-time in an office in Palmer Street, Darlinghurst. She left for work just before midday most days and returned at around six p.m. Well paid, she thought nothing of spoiling her lover with expensive gifts. Because she saw less of him than she liked, she suggested that he take a day job, perhaps making use of his trade. That way, they would have more time at night to spend together.

Harold heard that they were hiring painters to join the maintenance crew for the recently completed Sydney Harbour Bridge. He applied for the job and was hired. There weren't many willing applicants for work that required such a steely nerve. It involved working at great heights, sometimes suspended on trestles, which was much too daunting for some but not a problem for him. The job was permanent, provided that one was careful enough not to fall the several hundred feet to one's death. Harold had fallen from a trestle once before but didn't expect to do it again. There were several crews that, on a staggered schedule, painted from one end of the massive single-span bridge to the other and then repeated the entire process, continuously.

Harold stopped communicating with Dora. It was easier than telling her the truth. Dora wrote letters to Mollie pleading for any news of him. Harold didn't mention anything about Cathy to Mollie because he knew she wouldn't approve. He never brought anyone with him when he went to visit Mollie, and he refused to discuss his relationship with Dora. So all Mollie could suggest to Dora was that he'd simply moved on. She hated to believe it herself, such was her affection and regard for her brother's devoted, but evidently jilted, former girlfriend.

*

Nearly five years passed. Harold gradually became known to the police but only for minor matters such as the occasional pub or street brawl or for his cheeky, sometimes abrasive, attitude towards them. These offences were a long way down the list of importance for the police in a city as large as

Sydney but petty criminals such as Harold were still considered to be worth keeping an eye on.

He and Cathy had just returned from a fortnight's holiday at a resort hotel in the Blue Mountains, booked and paid for by her. It was her Christmas present to him. He hadn't bought a present for her. He had little time for the whole Christmas thing, normally spending the day alone, by choice. She was mystified by his sullenness, his unwillingness to relax and enjoy it with her, so she'd travel south to spend it with her family. He had no inclination to discuss his feelings about it. He didn't really understand them himself. Mollie would plead with him to have lunch with her and Lucy but to no avail. He just wanted to spend the day alone.

On their return from their holiday, Cathy finally decided to tell him the truth – which was that she'd been working as a prostitute at a brothel for the past six years. She'd been nervous most of the time that they'd been together, fearful that he might discover her deceit and confront her with it. She was unsure of how to tell him but she needn't have been concerned. He accepted her revelation with a dismissive shrug. When she told him she'd give it all away if he wanted her to, he said it wasn't of any concern to him. It was up to her what she wanted to do for a living.

The hard part over, she suggested that the smart thing for them to do was to rent a larger apartment so that they could live in one section and she could utilise the remainder to service her own private clientele. Many of the men whom she saw regularly at the brothel would prefer to see her privately. The arrangement would also allow her to earn more because she wouldn't have to pay a share of her takings to the brothel-keeper.

It seemed like a good plan. Harold kept his job painting the bridge and in his spare time he would help to seek out new clients, pimping for her. Many of her new customers became regulars, enamoured of Cathy's beauty and expertise.

The money was good. The living was easy. It couldn't possibly last.

The owner of the brothel where Cathy had previously worked was unhappy about losing one of his most popular, reliable and experienced employees. Concerned that she might have gone over to one of his competitors, he finally decided to investigate her situation. Incensed when he discovered that she was now working independently, he insisted that she return to work for him. Harold let him off with a minor thrashing, which proved to be a major mistake. The brothel-keeper visited the detective who'd been corruptly overseeing his protection from prosecution for many years. The pair was arrested.

Cathy was convicted and gaoled for operating a brothel. New legislation had recently been enacted that made 'consorting with known criminals' an offence. Before then, the closest thing they could have pinned on Harold would have been a charge of vagrancy, for which the punishment was a fine. On the twenty-eighth day of February 1935, he was sentenced to six months at hard labour in Long Bay Penitentiary, the first person to serve time in prison for the offence of consorting.

'The Bay' was a slightly more civilised prison than some but was still a tough gaol. On his charge sheet, Harold was careful to register his professions as painter and cook, although he'd never successfully cooked anything in his life. He'd been hoping to secure a job in the prison kitchen in order to have access to fresh, untainted food. An amazing number of crims gave their occupations as cooks. This time, he wasn't one of the lucky ones to get a coveted job in the kitchen – he'd been sentenced to hard labour, after all. Most of his waking hours were spent in the oppressive prison laundry. Open wood stoves provided the necessary heating, there was absolutely no automation and all washing and rinsing was done by hand.

His previous experience of prison life proved handy but he still had to fight for his place in the pecking order. He rapidly gained the respect of his peers and the 'sixer' passed with little drama.

After being released in July, he once more promised himself that he'd never again become a guest of the king. He was twenty-six years old and exhausted. The excitement of life in the big city had subsided. It was time to return home, to make the maximum effort to settle down and lead a normal life. He knew his old nemesis Sergeant Clark would be lying in wait for him to make even the slightest mistake. He'd have to be careful – smart – and not give him any opportunity.

He'd exchanged letters with Cathy for the first few months of their sentences and then gradually ceased contact. For him at least, the fire under their once passionate relationship had flickered, faltered and now died.

He sent Jock a telegram informing him of his impending return to Brisbane. He thought it was advisable to address the wire to Jock only. He couldn't really expect Dora to be all that keen to be there when he arrived, considering his earlier offhanded treatment of her.

He underestimated her. Dora was on the platform at South Brisbane station when he alighted. She'd asked Jock to give her this chance to welcome him home alone. Although he looked different – more thin and drawn – her feelings for him hadn't changed during the eight years since she'd last seen him. Her heart leapt at the sight of him. She loved him still. Nothing could ever change that.

Dora's welcome, and its effect on him, surprised him. There was no dramatic scene, simply a brief kiss and a hug, but his pulse was quickened by the undeniable warmth of her reception. He immediately felt completely at ease in her presence. It was as if they'd been apart for only a few short months. She by now had developed into a mature, attractive and confident young woman. She wore some makeup, not much, a stylish, brimmed felt hat and a tailored overcoat with fur collar, buttoned at the front, over her preferred floral cotton dress.

They walked and talked all of the way home to the Valley. There was so much that she wondered about but she asked only a few basic questions. He would tell her what he wanted her to know. She could accept that. There was no rush.

Dora had remained in her job as a machinist while Harold was away. Had she accepted the many offers of dates from the young men she met at the dances she still loved going to with Jock and Winnie, she'd have led a much busier social life. But she'd developed a strong belief that Harold would come back to her one day and she'd clung to it. She'd been proven right.

Harold noticed that she had matured not just in looks. Her attitude to Annie was respectful as always – she still lived beneath her mother's roof, after all – but she was more forthright with her than Harold remembered. It impressed him that she was demanding more respect for herself and her opinions. When she and Annie argued, which seemed to be fairly regularly, Dora demonstrated more strength and held her own more than before. She was now nobody's pushover.

20

The Proposal

Being unable to abolish love,
the Church ... has invented marriage

Charles Beaudelaire (1821–67)

Harold returned to painting and found work with a subcontractor. He moved back into Maggie's house, and he and Dora saw each other almost every evening. As the months passed, he surprised his mates and Dora, especially, with his resolve to keep some of his former uncivilised impulses under control. He calmed down so much that when he suggested, quite of the blue, that they should move into a place of their own, Dora didn't hesitate. She knew Annie wouldn't approve but she didn't care. She had her own life to lead and required no sanction from her mother as to how she should conduct it. At this point in her life, it was what she wanted more than anything.

Harold found a typical two-bedroom Queenslander to rent in Robert Street, Spring Hill. It wasn't long before some of the more sanctimonious gossips in the neighbourhood learned that the young couple weren't married, and they were suitably appalled. Harold and Dora's de facto lifestyle was considered bohemian and outlandish but neither could care less. Indeed, they found the prattle amusing. They simply wanted to keep to themselves and live their lives their own way. Annie, as anticipated, was deeply aggrieved and didn't hesitate to say so. For some reason that was difficult for Harold to fathom, she seemed to expect her daughter to display much higher moral standards than she herself had when she was young. It would be several years before Annie overcame her outrage and they all spoke again.

Jock had married Winifred. Brickie was married to Margaret, Johnno to Ellen and Irish was living with Edie. They were all expecting children. Tommy had been married for almost a year but his wife, Irene, had died from pneumonia in the latter stages of her first pregnancy. Their child couldn't be saved.

*

The Proposal

Harold was kept under close scrutiny by Knobby Clark. The copper, although he would never admit it at the time, was becoming more and more impressed with Harold's new attitude – but he didn't expect it to last. Young criminals like Harold Fingleton never, ever really reformed. Sergeant Clark was looking forward to the day when he'd be proven right.

It never arrived.

He was surprised to learn that the bloke whose life he'd fully expected would someday come to an untimely, violent end was a hard worker – never missed a day.

Harold had come to the realisation that it was up to him alone to take charge of his life. He avoided situations that might lead to trouble and was able, albeit a little grudgingly, to walk away from scenarios that would have resulted in physical mayhem in days past. He was becoming more and more satisfied and confident that the new lifestyle he was embracing might actually work for him.

Tommy was a very regular visitor. Dora, especially, always greeted him warmly and made an effort to ensure that he never felt as if he might be intruding in any way. It wasn't difficult for her. She loved company and besides, Tom was almost impossible to dislike. He would overcome the tragic loss of the only woman he'd ever loved but he would need the support of friends like Harold and Dora. He was at their place the afternoon that Dora returned from her doctor's appointment with the news that she was pregnant.

She'd long realised that Harold was no romantic but even she didn't expect his reaction to her excited, though tempered and hesitant, report. It was to remain in her memory forever.

'Pregnant, eh? Hmm,' Harold mused. 'S'pose we'd better get married. What do you think, Tommy?'

Tom looked blankly at Dora. Then back at Harold. Then back at Dora again. He was flabbergasted, struck instantly speechless. Why ask him? He attempted to offer an opinion, but no words, only an 'um' and an 'ah', would come.

Dora chuckled resignedly but she had wanted to become a mother for a long time. Nothing could spoil the moment for her. 'Well, I would have liked a more romantic proposal but I suppose that'll have to do!'

The marriage ceremony was performed by the registrar of births, deaths and marriages, in the government buildings at North Quay. Harold was twenty-nine, Dora twenty-six.

They rented a new three-bedroom house in Boundary Street, some four blocks along from Maggie.

News of Dora's pregnancy stirred Mollie into immediate action. She had come to terms with the fact that her brother and Dora had been living in sin – up until this point. Now she would have to step in. There were certain religious protocols that must still be addressed. A child must not be born out of Christian wedlock, for fear of bearing the eternal disgrace of being illegitimate, a bastard. Her Catholic beliefs gave no credence whatsoever to state marriages. They would have to be married 'in the eyes of the Church'. Dora wondered privately why the irony of her insistence, considering her own personal circumstances, apparently did not dawn on Mollie.

Had it been anyone else, Harold would have ignored such counsel and given suitable advice as to where the counsellor might shove it. But it came from Mollie, and Mollie would never give him the wrong advice as far as he was concerned. For Dora's part, she was irreligious and saw no point in objecting. It would make no difference to her either way.

So their union was consecrated in their living room – Dora heavily with child, Harold obediently and submissively resigned – by Father, soon to become Monseigneur Carlton. Mollie was suitably assuaged because their sinful living arrangements had been made sinless and life could now proceed in blessed style.

*

Harold was aware that certain permanent changes would have to take place in his life. With the responsibilities of fatherhood looming, he needed to make some promises to himself and to Dora, and needed to set himself some clear goals. The most important of these was to swear off the drink for good. He'd never be able to give his family his best if he didn't do that.

As well, he was determined to ensure that his offspring would never go hungry or suffer any of the other awful childhood experiences that he had. They should each have the advantage of a good education and be taught to be disciplined, well-behaved and law-abiding. In short, with Dora's support, he'd do his best to ensure that their lives would be nothing like his had been. He was destined to live in constant dread that his criminal past might, in some way or other, one day become a handicap to them. It never did.

Having steady employment was going to be essential, but his present work had a serious drawback. Harold had been suffering with severe tinea from the combination of the subtropical heat and the sandshoes he wore in his work as a painter. His feet would perspire profusely and were hardly ever dry, so it was nearly impossible to treat the fiercely itching complaint successfully. He left his trade behind and took employment as a wharf labourer, remaining in that job for the rest of his working life.

Harold and Dora's eldest child, Harold Thomas, was born in November 1938. A cheeky, athletic boy, he was given the nickname 'the Champ' at his birth – and from that moment forward would endeavour to impress his father with a toughness that lived up to that name.

When the Second World War broke out in Europe,

The Proposal

Australia's decision to support the British involvement was a given. Wharfies could join the armed forces but were exempt from compulsory call-up because theirs was an essential service – vital to the war effort. Supplies had to be shipped to all parts of the world where Australian defence forces were stationed and the men of the waterfront were needed to ensure that ships were swiftly and efficiently loaded.

Nevertheless, despite his exemption, Harold went to try to sign up, along with Tommy. The medical staff gave Harold the lowest rating, 4F. His pride dented, he consoled himself by deciding that the reason they'd declared him unfit for service was probably his police record – but he did recall one of the examining doctors commenting, 'This bloke even has flat feet.' Tommy was accepted and was to see action in the Middle East. The wharfies, Harold included, would pull their weight willingly and manfully during the war, double shifts being the normal order during those days of worldwide upheaval.

In April 1940, Dora gave birth to Anthony James, a sickly child who spent most of his early years under her watchful eye and on her hip. Tony suffered from almost every childhood malaise known but he survived them all. His grittiness was to become a hallmark of his character and he was destined for great achievements.

In the years that Harold had been away interstate, Dora had kept in regular touch with Maggie, who'd continued to live in the same house on Boundary Street. Dora had never developed any real fondness or respect for Harold's mother, never having been able to come to terms with the fact that she'd been so cruel to her son. It was beyond the scope of her maternal instinct to understand how any mother could treat her child in such a way, no matter what the circumstances. But the old woman's health was fading, so she suggested that they take her in to look after her, and Harold agreed. Maggie died in her sleep in 1942, aged eighty, having remained sober for twenty years. Her passing was of no great consequence to her son, on the surface, although he was never heard to utter a word of criticism about her and would visit her grave site with flowers every few months for the rest of his life.

John Alan, the middle pin, was born in October 1943, a couple of months prematurely. Dora feared that he could be her second miscarriage – she had suffered one eighteen months previously. She needn't have been concerned. After a breech delivery and the jaundice that often accompanies premmie births, he developed into a healthy, robust child. From early in his life, he showed both an eager appreciation for his food and the impatience that he'd demonstrated with his early arrival.

The fourth boy was Ronald Graham, born in May 1945, lively and eternally energetic and playful. His lust for excitement and boisterous fun caused him to experience

The Proposal

many minor injuries and close calls during his childhood and he was a constant worry to the rest of the family.

In January 1947, Dora gave birth to the last of five children. She'd given up all hope of delivering a baby girl and when her doctor informed her that she'd finally given birth to a daughter, she rebuked him, saying: 'Please don't crack jokes with me, Doctor, I'm too tired.' Diane Maryellen – a pretty little girl, with long brown hair and blue eyes like her siblings – rounded out the quintet perfectly. She was cute and demanding of her mother's attention, which was given generously, as with the rest. She also was destined for fame.

If it had been possible financially, Dora would've loved to have had several more children but they were going to have a battle to get the job done as it was.

*

Harold enjoyed the working environment on the wharf. There, as on the docks of Melbourne, people kept their own counsel and minded their own business. A man's past was never inquired into and any transgression of this rule was viewed with suspicion and earned the inquirer short shrift.

There was a widely held belief that the wharves were a haven for Communists, who were thought to emerge from the extreme left wing of the Labor Party. Certainly, there was a substantial Communist element among the wharfies but Harold despised them. He was a Labor man and a socialist but never, ever a 'commo'. To his mind, there was a difference, one that was clear to reasonable, sensible thinkers but rarely acknowledged. He believed in the working man's right to strike for better pay and conditions. But if a man had the necessary ability and acumen to build a business of his own, he was to be respected and admired for it. Harold was more than happy for there to be bosses and workers – and clearly defined lines of demarcation between the two – as long as the employees were shown some respect as well. As with most facets of his life, he knew exactly where he stood and it would take a convincing argument to dissuade him from that position, no matter who was proposing it.

The work that the wharfies performed offered variety but was mostly arduous, sometimes dangerous and always extremely tiring. Apart from the huge winches that were used to remove cargo from the ships' holds, there was little in the way of mechanical assistance. The labourers sometimes were called 'wharf lumpers' because they would physically carry, or lump, bags of wheat and other produce on their shoulders and manhandle bales of wool with the aid of grappling hooks. The blade of a grappling hook – sharpened to a fine point at the end, and roughly fifteen inches long and half an inch in diameter – was usually bolted through a wooden crossbar handle. A man held the handle and placed the blade

The Proposal

between his middle and ring finger. Outbreaks of violence were not uncommon amongst the mostly tough types who found their way into this industry and use of the hooks was by no means barred during altercations. Harold, as was now his habit, avoided all personal confrontations. He had nothing to prove to anyone and wasn't expected to do so.

Occasionally, a crate of produce would 'accidentally' break open and most of the men would help themselves to their share. Harold never did, because spot checks were occasionally conducted at the exit gate. Every now and then, however, a 'gift' would appear on his doorstep – often some export-quality beef – and he and his family would eat well. The wharfies had a way of caring for and sharing with those among them whom they liked and admired. He mixed with a small, respected clique of experienced hands who sat together and chatted during smokos and lunch breaks or dangled a line over the side of the wharf, usually futilely. The Brisbane River notoriously surrendered minimal quantities of its marine life.

Among that clique was a fellow named Freddie Davis, an ex-professional boxer who, unlike Harold, was keen to partake in any rorts that were afoot and never hesitated to fight when even slightly provoked. His bad temper was legendary but his and Harold's relationship revolved mainly around discovering good-humoured ways to get under each other's skin. Fred was known for his penchant for practical jokes and he delighted in making Harold the butt of them whenever possible. Reciprocal rights were respected and retaliation in kind expected.

During one midnight shift, Harold had dangled the usual supremely optimistic fishing line over the side of the ship. He would leave his rod unattended most of the time, secured to the ship's rail. While Harold was occupied with work, Fred furtively hauled the line from the water and attached to it a piece of tin, bent at the corners, that he'd cut from the bottom of a five-gallon drum. Then he cast it back into the briny. Under the moonlight, shimmering just below the surface, it looked exactly like a large bream, one of the few types of fish that might possibly be expected to be caught in the river. He positioned himself beside his mate's rod.

'Harold, Harold, quick, quick, I think you've caught something!' he yelled urgently, at the same time attracting the attention of most of their workmates. They all realised Freddie had been busy setting up one of his specialist pranks.

Harold was on the spot in a flash. 'You bloody little beauty, finally got one! Jesus, it looks like a good 'un, Freddie!' Playing up to his audience, Harold then demonstrated his brilliant technique in playing the 'fish': drawing it in, releasing the tension in the line, back and forth, before finally landing it onto the deck.

The Proposal

before the truth dawned on him. Fred and the rest of work gang number 87 were by this time legless with merriment.

Harold spent the next few minutes apprising his pal of his opinion of his parentage and instructing him as to where he should go and what he should do when he arrived there – with suitable adjectives succinctly interspersed.

Fred had a son, young Freddie, who also came to work on the wharves. A short, slightly built, quietly spoken lad of the most disarmingly gentle manner, he was polite and respectful of his older workmates. His demeanour was most misleading, for he, too, had been a successful professional boxer, though he never went out of his way to demonstrate his skills. Indeed, his temperament was the opposite of Fred senior's – always under control. Young Freddie had left school at age fourteen.

Harold admired the lad tremendously and when Freddie senior died prematurely from a heart attack, he took a deep interest in his life. He recognised in the youngster an intellect at least the equal of any of his own children, all of whom, except for Harold junior, would have far more extensive schooling than young Fred. Young Freddie read avidly, some of the literature beyond the scope of Harold to grasp. It set him apart from the rest of the workforce on the wharves.

Harold set about planting the seed in young Freddie's mind that he was capable of better things than a career on the wharves. His months of nagging convinced the younger fellow that he should go back and complete his secondary school education. This accomplished, with excellent marks, he studied at the Teachers Training College. Fred became a secondary school teacher and continued to pursue a life of study, specialising in languages. He remains ever mindful of, and thankful for, his mentor's encouragement.

*

Harold had become a zealous Labor Party supporter. At election times he displayed prominent 'Vote 1' signs in the front yard in support of the local member for the seat of Brisbane, Johnno Mann. Johnno was a regular visitor at 490 Boundary Street and would take the children for a spin in his government-issue limousine most Sunday mornings. His career was on an upward spiral and he would eventually be appointed speaker of the Queensland parliament, a position that he would hold for nearly eight years. He had progressed in admirable fashion from his days as a builder's labourer.

Harold became a committed trade unionist. The fatality rate amongst wharf labourers was the highest by far of any industry in those times. Wharfies were denied basic rights, such as the provision of first aid and even washroom and toilet facilities and they made meagre livings. In New South Wales and Victoria, wharfies earned half as much again as their counterparts in Queensland.

As a result, there was ongoing conflict between the wharf labourers and the shipping companies. Once the war, with all of its horror and loss of life, had ended, the wharfies turned to strike action as the only effective method to achieve reasonable wages and safe, hygienic working conditions.

The news media of the day generally supported the interests of the wealthy shipowners and portrayed the wharfies as Communists and layabouts, more interested in causing trouble than performing their duties. The vast majority of them were like Harold, of course: hard workers with families to support and rent to pay who could ill afford to lose valuable working hours. But they had to display a united front or they would continue to be exploited, walked over and trodden on. A slush fund was provided by the Waterside Workers Federation that those in urgent need could draw upon during strikes. Somehow, all would manage to battle their way through until work resumed. Dora and Harold always seemed to be able to manage to provide for their kids. Certainly, the children sat down to healthy and plentiful meals even during the most lengthy work stoppages.

Even when it was clear that the employers were in the wrong, they would hold out against the strikers' demands, determined to make life as difficult as possible for the men whose endeavours kept them wealthy. At the end of a strike, generous overtime rates had to be paid to redress the backlog of freight, so often there were no winners or losers after all.

When the shipowners became desperate, with cargo to move and ships backing up towards the mouth of the Brisbane River, they would resort to employing scab labour, a tactic that was anathema to strikers. Though violence was a last, desperate resort avoided by both sides, when scabs were brought in, riotous conflict would sometimes break out. The entrances to the wharves would become scenes of extraordinary physical confrontation, with vicious hand-to-hand combat between striking workers on the one side, and scabs and hired henchmen (generally unemployed people plucked from pubs and country towns) on the other.

For Harold, there was no other option but to join in. Solidarity demanded his involvement. Dora understood that. His awareness and the experience of so many brawls in the streets of the Valley in his youth stood by him. He would survive virtually unscathed but there were, of course, many injuries on both sides after each melee. Almost miraculously, there were no fatalities, at least not in Brisbane. On the wharves in Fremantle, Western Australia, in 1919, a man named Edwards had been killed; and in 1928, Alan Whittaker, a Gallipoli veteran, was shot in the back of the head and killed during a riot against scabs in Melbourne.

Police, many on horseback, would intervene to restore control. Arrests were made very rarely, though, for fear of political backlash from all quarters. More often than not, the outcome was eventually decided diplomatically by the worker-friendly State Labor government of the day. An unsteady peace would reign until the next dispute arose.

One of the lengthiest strikes by wharfies took place in 1949, when they went out in sympathy with tram and bus drivers and conductors, to provide extra clout to their demands for better wages. The drivers and conductors weakened within days and the wharfies were left to carry the dispute to its successful conclusion over a period of many weeks. The tram and bus workers were for a number of years regarded as weak by many fellow unionists as a result of what was construed as a cave-in. As far as Harold and most of his workmates were concerned, they could hardly expect any respect if they weren't willing to stand up for themselves.

One of the most far-reaching and important initiatives undertaken by the union movement at this time was for a selfless cause. In 1942, the Dutch had shown little or no resistance to Japanese forces when they invaded the Netherlands East Indies, which had been a Dutch colony for more than three centuries. Within weeks, the Dutch administration sought, and was given, refuge in Australia. At the conclusion of the war, the Dutch were determined to regain the East Indies from the local Indonesians by force.

The Australian populace by and large was sympathetic towards any country's struggle for independence from colonial control. Indeed, many Australian prisoners of war had forged strong friendships with Indonesian 'volunteers' who were forced to slave alongside them in their thousands during construction of the infamous Burma-to-Thailand railway.

The first of many marches in support of a black ban on Dutch ships was conducted by the Brisbane branch of the Waterside Workers Federation early in 1946. The ban soon garnered support from unionists in Sydney, Melbourne and Adelaide, initially, and then New Zealand, Canada, North America and several other countries on the Pacific rim. The virtually worldwide boycott ensured that in excess of 550 Dutch vessels remained at anchor, effectively immobilising any possible war effort against the Indonesians. In most places, ships were denied access to ports even for repairs. The embargo remained in place until 1948. Independence for the Indonesian people from Dutch colonial rule was the end game and the country was recognised and acknowledged as a republic by the Dutch Government in late 1949.

Approaches had been made to Harold in an effort to have him become a union official but he declined. He was more than willing to take part in any worthwhile protest march, however, and did so, often welcomed to the front ranks.

21
Turning Mugs into Men

You can tell a mug – but you can't tell him anything

Anonymous

In the years immediately following the war, there was no shortage of budding gangsters among the youngsters that roamed the streets of Spring Hill. Mid-to-late teenage lads, some of them had suffered the loss of fathers killed during the conflict; others came from poor families made poorer by common frailties such as alcoholism and gambling. Few had any decent education to which to lay claim. Harold got to know them all and they liked him because he seemed to understand them. Sometimes, he seemed to know what they were thinking but he never made a big thing out of it. Certainly, he never tried to talk down to them or give them any unwanted or unsought advice. Small lively, cheeky groups of them would join him when he walked home from work or call, uninvited but always welcome, at the house to chat about their lives and their problems.

Harold might've been at work but Dora was always cheerfully hospitable. They could always be assured of an uncommonly worldly, sympathetic and gentle understanding of their troubles from her. She readily recognised familiar patterns emerging within some of them. Many were developing attitudes that would point them down the same path that her husband had travelled himself an age ago. Most appeared to despise any form of authority and already had begun to drink heavily or to embrace criminality in one form or another.

One afternoon, Harold was moved to say, 'You know, Dora, most of these young lairs aren't bad kids. One or two might be a handful but most of 'em just need somethin' to occupy their time, keep 'em busy. A few of 'em are gunna end up in boob for sure if someone doesn't do something to help 'em.'

'Why don't you?' She waited for a response.

'Me! What could I do?' he fired back.

'Well, these boys look up to you. I think that if you took some of them under your wing, you might be able to do them some good.'

'How could I do 'em any good?' He'd like to think that it

might be possible but he had never seen himself as any kind of role model.

'Well, maybe you could teach them to play football or something. Why don't you have a talk to Johnno? See if you can't work out something with him. You'd think he'd have some ideas, wouldn't he?' Dora always saw things with more clarity than her husband did. More important than anything else, to her, was the need for eternal vigilance on her part; she had to remain alert for any small indication of a weakening of his resolve to stay off the drink. She was aware of the daily battle that he fought with his will.

Harold absorbed her words. She noticed that his brow lifted and his eyes widened slightly as he slowly nodded his head. His mind began to fairly race. Not only would he be able to do something for the youngsters but he could put some of his dormant sporting expertise to good use. It was exciting to him.

So the next time he had a night shift and time to spare during the day, he called in to see Johnno at his place. Johnno still lived in the family home on St Paul's Terrace. His parents had passed away years previously and had left the house to him.

The Member for Brisbane embraced the idea with all of the vigour for which he was renowned. Apart from anything else, it would be good for him politically. He was always eager to consider any plan that might lead to less lawlessness in his electorate. It wouldn't be difficult to talk members of the local business community into providing logistical support for the plan. They were the ones with most to lose from burglaries and the like. The actual teaching and training aspects he would leave to Harold, who knew from experience the feeling of well-being and satisfaction to be gained from fitness training, and how team competition had the potential to develop character and a cooperative spirit.

The difficult part would be to get the lads involved. Harold had detected some leadership qualities in two of them in particular, Len Johnstone and Johnny Turner. He sent a message to them that he'd like to get together and talk about something. The boys arrived at Harold's place and, as usual, they were made welcome and offered something to eat and drink by Dora. Within minutes, the group was sitting at the kitchen table enjoying sandwiches and tea.

Harold told them what he had spoken about with Johnno. The two youngsters seemed reticent at first but gradually warmed to the idea. He said that he would need their assistance, that he saw them as potential leaders who could help him to get the rest interested. Their self-esteem suitably buoyed by Harold's assessment of them, they agreed to his next suggestion heartily. The following Friday, Johnno and Harold would supply a keg of beer, Dora would prepare some food and Len and Johnny would gather as many of the lads who might be interested, for a discussion about the idea. Perhaps the young men would've jumped from the Storey Bridge if Harold had asked them to, but he was thrilled with how willing they were to help.

Johnno invited Pat Scanlan, the owner of the City View Hotel, up on Leichhardt Street, to attend. He generously supplied a keg free of charge – most of the young men drank regularly at his pub, after all. The free beer may have been the main attraction for some, but a larger-than-expected group of about twenty, plus Scanlan, Johnno and the Fingleton clan, squeezed into the dining room, kitchen and back verandah of 490 Boundary Street the following Friday evening.

Harold explained his proposal: if he could get enough of them interested, they would set up their own club, which would be registered with the Brisbane Rugby League. They would apply to be accepted into one of the minor competitions initially. They would have their own colours and uniforms. The patron of the club would be Mr Mann, whom all knew well, and the secretary, treasurer and coach would be Harold himself. A show of hands was requested. Boozy camaraderie bolstered the number of yeses and at the end of the night's carousing, a tentative arrangement had been agreed to. Training would start the following Thursday at five-thirty p.m. at Normanby Oval.

In the meantime, Harold advised them, it might serve them well to start jogging as a means towards achieving some basic fitness. As many as could afford them should supply their own boots, socks and shorts. Those who couldn't – and that was the majority – should let Harold know by Monday morning and he would set about gathering together as much equipment as he could beg or borrow – legally these days. He made one thing clear to each and every one of them: if any of them gave a commitment to turn up for training or matches, he'd better bloody well do so, or suffer the consequences. It was left to their own imaginations what those consequences might be. It was probably not a good idea to have Harold waste his time and effort.

The first training run, if it could be described as that, proved to be a comical fiasco. Apart from four or five of the group who seemed to be blessed with some natural athleticism and potential football talent, the remainder were a disheartening, gormless bunch of awkward fumblers, entirely bereft of any discernible timing or coordination. Harold would have to start from the very beginning and teach them the most basic skills: carrying, catching and passing the ball, tackling, gathering a rolling ball, punting and drop-kicking. A select few would be coached in the art of place-kicking, because if the team did play well enough to score any tries, they'd need to have a good goal kicker to convert them. There would be no football matches in the foreseeable future for this lot – only practice, practice and more practice.

Harold arrived home from his initial coaching experience

mentally exhausted and frustrated but pleased, at least, with the cheerful attitude that the lads had displayed. A few of the group might've been hopeless cases but all seemed willing to listen and learn. He couldn't wait for the next session, which was set down for the following Saturday morning at ten o'clock. He realised that he was tempting fate with the timing. Most of the lads normally spent Saturday morning in recovery from the stresses of Friday night. But he was very interested to see who'd turn up and who wouldn't. It was the first of many tests that he'd set his charges in order to get some indication of their true potential.

It was just before ten when he arrived at the oval, which was about a fifteen-minute walk from home. To his surprise and delight, half a dozen of his boys were already there, laughing and skylarking and skiting about the doings and conquests of the previous evening. Another ten or so arrived on foot or on pushbike and within half an hour, training had begun.

Soon they had settled into a system of thrice-weekly training, on Tuesdays, Thursdays and Saturdays. One of the lads, Keith Doyle, impressed his coach with his tremendous speed. He was a rather handsome fellow and was well aware of it. He was always concerned that his thick black hair should at all times remain tidy and was at pains to turn out at training with his gear pressed and spotless. Harold thought he would make a perfect winger, as long as he could teach the lad to hang on to the bloody ball instead of dropping, throwing or kicking the thing away at the first sign that he might be tackled. He devised a plan: if Doyle experienced the thrill of actually scoring a try, he might become more determined to take a risk or two. After a loosening-up canter a couple of times around the oval, Harold instructed his charges to form two groups of equal number. They were going to have a practice match. He then called aside Len Johnstone, who would be 'marking' Doyle.

'Lennie,' he said confidentially, 'as soon as the ball looks like getting to Doyley in the open, I want you to give him clear running. I don't care how you do it – trip over if you have to – but I want him to score a try. Okay?'

'Yeah, Harold, I get it.'

He then spoke to Keith. 'Doyley, next time you get the ball with any room to move, I want you to stick it under your arm and run as fast as you can and keep goin', all right?'

Doyle nodded his comprehension, at the same time tidying a few unruly strands of his hair.

Within minutes, the perfect scenario developed. Johnstone, as arranged, 'slipped' as soon as Keith received the ball. Keith was off with flashing speed – down the field, past the fullback, across the tryline, over the fence, up the hill to the Normanby Fiveways intersection and away, out of sight, to roars of encouragement from his team-mates and a stinging tirade of abuse from his coach.

'Come back, come back, ya bastard – that's the only ball we've got!' he screamed. His plea was ignored.

The rest of the team paid a price for their encouragement of the rogue winger: seemingly endless laps of the oval. Finally, Harold called time and they made their way, as they usually did after training, back to the City View for a few refreshing beers.

Pat Scanlan was happy to occasionally shout his best customers a couple of free ones. Harold would join them for a lemonade or double sarsaparilla. The players, aware of his reputation as a big drinker when he was young, could barely believe it but were deeply impressed with his resolve. The group arrived at the hotel and there at the bar – grinning widely, beer in hand – stood one Keith Doyle, his arm casually resting on the football with which he'd absconded.

'What'd you think you were doin', ya bludger?' Harold asked.

'You told me to put this thing under me arm and keep runnin' and I did!' his winger replied.

'Yeah, but only as far as the bloody tryline!' Harold rebuked him, with feigned annoyance. He gave them all the impression that he didn't see the funny side of the matter but he certainly did – he could hardly wait to get home and tell Dora about it. Doyley would have to pay a premium for his disappearing act at the next training session, however.

For the team's uniform, Harold successfully applied for permission to use a version of the royal blue colours of the club he had played for when he was young, the Fortitude Valley Diehards. Their jersey had a simple, one-colour design with a white badge above the left breast and white numbering. Pat Scanlan had developed a keen involvement in Harold's venture and willingly covered the bill for the uniforms. In appreciation for his support, the team would be called the City Views. The Brisbane Rugby League accepted them into the D grade, as they were a fledgling club.

It took many weeks of frustration and hard work before Harold felt that his charges were anywhere near ready for any proper competition. To give his newcomers some kind of experience of actual match conditions, he set about trying to arrange a few midweek practice games with teams already playing in minor comps. He located a coach who was happy for his players to have an easy match instead of the dreary, repetitious training run that they were used to. However, it quickly degenerated into an all-in brawl. The very first tackle by one of the opposition players was seen by the Spring Hill mob as an unreasonable act of aggression and raised their ire. The game was called off before it had really begun and it took some time for a semblance of order to be restored.

Harold was duly informed by the opposition coach what he should do with his 'team of ratbags'. He could hardly take exception. He realised that they had a bit to learn about the basics of fair physical competition.

But learn they did. Over the ensuing months, they progressed in ability and teamwork sufficiently to not only enter the D-grade competition but reach the grand final. The night before, they were all looking forward excitedly to the showdown as they gathered at the Fingleton house for the usual free keg of beer. Harold saw it as the lesser of two evils to have his charges around to drink on the night before a game. At least he knew where they were. He and Johnno had quickly grown tired of having to bail out half of them on match-day morning. This was a popular solution to that problem.

The grand final was a good close match. With the City Views down by two points in the dying stages, a brilliant break down the left side of the field by fullback 'Skinny' Locke set up an overlap for Doyley. Given the ball with thirty yards to run to the tryline, Doyle set off apace. The opposition fullback was all but outrun – then in a desperate lunge, he dived and grasped Doyley's shorts. The shorts and his jockstrap ripped apart at the seams, leaving the winger naked from the waist down. He faltered in his stride.

'Don't let that worry ya! Keep goin', keep goin', Doyley, ya bludger!' screamed Harold, loud enough to be heard well above the din of the shrieking, highly amused spectators.

But to no avail. Doyley, absolutely, totally embarrassed, stopped running, sank to his knees in an effort to cover his nakedness and was swiftly swamped by defenders. The game was lost but no grudges would be carried. Doyley would have to live forever, though, with the good-natured jibes from the team-mates whom he had cost a premiership.

Harold decided that a function should be held to present trophies to the team to celebrate their successful season and reward his players for their efforts and perseverance. With Dora's assistance, he was able to conceive of a reason to award each and every one an accolade. Many a mantel would be decorated that evening, and for many years to come, with evidence of its owner's proud achievement.

Before the beginning of the next season, Pat Scanlan decided to sell the City View and purchase another pub not far away, at the Normanby Fiveways. The new owner of the City View was happy to sponsor the football team but wanted one of his mates to take over the coaching job.

The new pub owner was left with no players and no club – Harold's team would never train or play for anyone else. Harold set up another club for them. This one was called the Valley All Whites and it remained in existence for the next four years. Over that period, they competed in the grand final each season but failed to win one.

The day came when it was time for most of the players to focus on getting on with their adult lives. The original plan had worked almost to perfection. There was hardly a blemish on the police records of any of the players during those years and most of the troublemakers were now more settled. Many had found jobs or become apprentices in various trades and Harold was able to organise work on the wharves for those who wanted it. The young men would visit the Fingletons with their new girlfriends, some to proudly announce their engagements. Harold, Dora and Johnno were forced to acknowledge failure with the odd one or two – some remained unchanged despite their best efforts – but they could rightly feel proud of what they'd achieved.

*

When someone at work suggested over lunch one day that it might be a good idea to start a waterside workers' cricket club, Harold embraced the idea enthusiastically. It would give him the chance again to play his second-favourite sport and to keep busy during the summer months.

There were more than enough willing players and Harold was appointed captain and secretary-treasurer, though he was to relinquish the honour of being captain early in the piece because of his workload. The irony in the fact that an old thief was now treasurer of a sporting club was not lost on him – but times had changed and so had he. The trade union was more than willing to get involved and sponsored the cost of most of the cricket gear. Within weeks, the Waterside

Workers' Cricket Club was playing its first match. There were plenty of business and social clubs with which to have matches and the first season was a busy and enjoyable one.

It came to Harold's attention that there was a police social club team. When he made inquiries and discovered that Knobby Clark was one of the officials and played regularly, he wasted no time in arranging a match. It was to become a biannual event. Known colloquially as the Cops versus the Robbers, it was a day of light-hearted banter, bouncers and beam balls, delivered at gentle pace. In the earlier days of violent conflict between wharfies and police over scab labour, it would have been laughable to suggest that a friendly contest of this type would be possible. Harold's confrontation with Clark on and off the cricket field was good-natured; their past conflicts, on the surface anyway, had been consigned to history.

Interstate trips were organised, the Queensland and New South Wales branches of the Waterside Workers Federation playing annually in each other's home state. Annual wharfies' sporting carnivals became a highly popular spin-off.

Harold was also invited to play for the North Brisbane Pastimes Cricket Club, which he captained for four happy, busy years. At the end of that period, he realised that with his own family responsibilities becoming more and more demanding, it was time to hand over his duties to someone else.

22

The Tomato Fight

As he was valiant, I honour him.
But as he was ambitious, I slew him

Brutus, *Julius Caesar*,
William Shakespeare

The time would come when Harold was forced to renege on one of his promises to Dora. Apart from his earlier involvement in the violent strike action, he'd managed to steer clear of any kind of trouble. Then, he'd had her blessing – indeed, she would have been disappointed if he hadn't stood up for his beliefs.

Now came a different kind of challenge to his vow. It came at the conclusion of a typically exhausting day's work.

It was autumn, 1952. He was forty-three, still retained a full head of healthy (although greying) hair, and had by now not taken a drink for fourteen years. He was strong and fit for his age and loved the role of provider, husband and father.

Across the laneway from their house was a cement-rendered brick duplex that housed two shops, one a fish and chip shop, the other a grocery store. An Englishman named Victor Hill had taken the lease on the grocery store and moved into the cramped living quarters at the rear with his wife and small son. In his early thirties, tall, muscular and ruggedly handsome, Hill would drink most afternoons at the International Hotel, which was on the corner some one hundred yards from his shop, on the opposite side of the street. He lost no time in informing everyone interested – and many who were not – that he had been the middleweight champion of the British Armed Forces and had done a fair bit of professional boxing as well. Before long he had alienated himself from the regulars at the pub, many of whom were workmates and old friends of Harold's and, like him, despised pommies, as tradition demanded. Hill was too experienced and too skilled for any of the bar patrons who were silly enough to fall for his baiting and shape up to fight him. They found themselves dispatched to unconscious oblivion in quick time. He soon learned that Harold Fingleton had long been regarded as the best and most respected knuckle man in the area but nobody had seen him fight for years. Hill was keen to make a name for himself. He set about mounting a challenge.

The Tomato Fight

Dora did most of her shopping at Hill's store. Though she'd never had a problem with him before, he started being rude to her now and then. She tried to ignore it, certain that he must simply be having a bad day. Harold, who would occasionally buy his tobacco at the store on his way to and from work, noticed a change in Hill's attitude as well. His self-taught expertise in 'wiping a mug' – ignoring someone when it suited him – stood Harold in good stead. He suggested to Dora that she start doing her grocery shopping at the store a couple of hundred yards up Boundary Street in the opposite direction and she was happy to. She told the kids to do the same whenever she sent them on an errand.

Dora was hanging a sheet on the clothesline in the yard one day when she was struck on the back of the head. It stung, then something splattered across the sheet. Momentarily stunned, she wiped her head with her hand and saw that she had been struck by a tomato. Dora raised her fingers to her nose and found that it was a rather rotten, smelly one at that. She spun around to see where it had come from and saw Hill standing on the other side of the paling fence that separated his property from the Fingletons'. He didn't speak but the arrogant grin on his face said enough. He simply nodded at her and walked away.

Dora went up the back stairs to the kitchen. Diane, who had been running a temperature and was having a day at home from school, was sitting at the table doing some watercolouring in a colouring book. Dora went to the bathroom to run a warm bath to try to settle herself down. She was shaking and crying with shock and bewilderment.

She was only too aware of the awkwardness of her situation. She had two simple, clear-cut options: to tell Harold or not. Her first inclination was to keep the incident to herself. Why take the risk of stirring up trouble? She cleaned the mess from her hair in the hand basin and stepped into the tub. The water was soothing and sedating but she couldn't stop her tears from flowing. She felt anguished.

What was she to do?

She closed her eyes and told herself to relax, to think rationally.

Her thoughts gradually wandered back to the first days of her relationship with Harold. She recalled how she had loved him from the first moment. How his swaggering confidence in himself and his attitude of reckless disrespect for all authority had excited her. How she had come to respect and admire his principle of unconditional loyalty to those closest to him. How he had been such a show-off and always so handsome that she wondered what it was that he saw in her.

The feeling of warmth that her memories brought didn't last. She wept again as she recalled the unhappy stories of his treatment by his mother and the constant beatings and

The Tomato Fight

lack of care at St Vincent's. She recalled his travails at the hands of his tormentor, Knobby Clark; how it had hardened him and forced him to move away for the longest time. She recalled his sad confessions to her of his struggles to survive during those years, and how, ever since, there had been discernible unpleasant changes in the way he acted. Although he demonstrated great gentleness and love for their children, which caused pride and happiness to surge within her, he was lately more often given to fits of bad temper over the smallest and most unimportant of issues.

She sat upright in the bath, the water now beginning to chill, and chided herself to come to her senses. She hadn't often allowed herself the luxury of self-pity and she reminded herself of her duty to make the most of everything for the sake of their marriage and the secure future of the children.

Her problem now was to deal with the situation at hand. She saw clearly that she really had only one option. She must tell Harold what had happened and let him decide what, if any, course of action he wished to take. If she didn't tell him, he would surely find out about Hill's actions from someone else. Hill would see to it. She could imagine him standing at the bar of the hotel and branding Fingleton a dog and a coward for not fighting to protect his wife.

Harold arrived from work a little later than usual, having saved the few pennies for his bus fare by walking the two miles or so from the wharf at which his gang was currently working – Petrie Bight, at the far end of Boundary Street. Every little saved expense helped to feed his hungry brood. It had been a hard day and he was very tired. He rested on the bench of the hall stand at the entrance to the dining room for a few moments to catch his breath. His 'wind' wasn't as good as it used to be. All of the tobacco that he'd smoked over the years was taking its toll. He sat, striking a familiar pose – leaning forward, his elbows resting on his knees, fingers intertwined, breathing deeply. John, now eight years old, sat close beside him. He was most often the first to welcome him home.

'G'day, Dad.'

He ruffled his adoring son's hair. 'G'day, son, how're you goin'?'

'G'day, Dad,' chorused the rest.

'G'day, kids.'

He looked at Dora. The look on her face told him that there was a problem. Immediately, he scanned the room for his eldest son, expecting that any trouble would be his doing. Usually, it was.

'Harold,' his wife began, 'I know I've got to tell you this, but I wish I hadn't.'

'Shit, what is it?' He dreaded for a moment what the youngster might have accomplished during his travels this time. Dora usually didn't make such a big deal of this sort

The Tomato Fight

of thing. 'What's he done this time,' he asked, 'burned the bloody school down or somethin'?'

'No, no,' she reassured him. 'It's Hill, next door. He hit me in the head with a rotten tomato today.' Almost apologetically, she added, 'I didn't say a word to him, Harold, honestly. I was just hanging out some washing and he threw it at me. I haven't got a clue why he would do such a thing.'

Harold knew why. The experiences of a lifetime told him why. He looked up at Dora, shaking his head ever so slightly. No words were exchanged, nor were they necessary. Her reticent, almost unperceivable nod signalled to him that she understood what he had to do, even if she wished he did not.

'Oh well,' he said – and that was all he said.

With a small, tired grunt, he stood up, took off his work jacket, rolled up his shirtsleeves and retraced his steps along the hallway to the front door, down the front stairs and out onto the footpath, tracked closely by a deeply concerned Dora. Harold junior sensed what might be about to happen and followed them excitedly, close behind; the other children trailed timidly at the rear. Harold walked the twenty or so paces to the front door of Hill's store and, not wanting to enter the place, rapped his knuckles on the plate-glass shop window.

Hill was gathering some fruit from a basket for a customer. Harold's knock drew his delighted attention. He instantly removed his apron and scurried out to the footpath. At last his chance had come.

'So, you've turned up, 'ave you, ya grey-haired old bastard!'

Harold's retort was terse, self-assured, threatening. 'Don't let the grey hair fool you, son.'

Albert 'Sonny' Lawrence, a longtime neighbour from a few houses up the street, was on his way home from his regular afternoon visit to the International. It was rumoured that Sonny washed only rarely and never changed out of his pyjamas but during the day simply donned a pair of overalls over them and a pair of sandshoes. He sometimes wore a set of ill-fitting dentures, usually not. He saw what was about to happen and raced, as quickly as his unsteady legs could carry him, back to the public bar of the hotel.

'Fingo's about to go orf!' he spluttered to the drinkers and quickly retraced his steps to the scene at the front of the grocery shop. He was pursued within moments by a throng of some fifty or so spectators. This was going to be worth seeing.

By the time they'd arrived, only a few cautious straight lefts had been exchanged. Harold was showing his opponent due respect. By reputation alone, he was entitled to that. His normal routine had always been to throw as many punches as possible and get the job done as quickly as he could. But he could tell from the very way Hill shaped up that he knew what he was on about. The pair circled one another, content

The Tomato Fight

to let the other take the first risk, perhaps to leave an opening for a counterattack.

From the corner of his eye, Harold noticed Dora snatching at the peroxided hair of Hill's wife. Unbeknown to him, she had been about to bash Harold from behind with a broom that she'd brought from the shop. Dora and the flailing woman lost their balance and fell to the ground, screaming at each other. Two of the men from the hotel restrained one woman each.

While all of this was happening, Hill crashed a perfect right cross onto Harold's temporarily unguarded jaw. The blow made him weak at the knees. As he commenced to fall backwards, a left hook that might otherwise have lifted his head off whistled over it, missing its mark. Harold struggled to regather his senses and his balance and thrust out his right hand behind him. He used it as a fulcrum to swivel back to his full height, ready to resume combat. His head cleared quickly. He'd always been able to absorb punishment. Hill hesitated momentarily, impressed with and a little staggered by Fingleton's recovery rate. His right cross had swiftly concluded many previous conflicts for him.

'Jesus, Dora, will you turn it up!' Harold demanded. He had enough to handle without distractions. Her immediate instinct was to inform him in no uncertain terms that she'd just saved him a whack across the skull with a broom but she decided, under the current circumstances, to let the matter slide for the time being.

Hill's opening gambit loosened up both of them, and for the next few minutes, flurries of blows, jabs, left rips and hooks, right uppercuts and crosses were thrown by each from balanced stances, most finding their targets with that crisp slapping sound of knuckle on flesh exclusive to bare-fisted combat. A spontaneous hiss escaped each man's lips with almost every punch that he threw. Body blows that reached their mark were acknowledged with involuntary grunts of pain, some louder than others, depending upon their accuracy and strength.

'Come on, Harold.'

'Give it to 'im, Fingo!'

The support was one-sided, but the stoush wasn't.

Harold was beginning to feel terribly tired. Hill, putting the boxing adage 'Kill the body and the head dies' into effect, was directing plenty of his punches to Harold's body. A good fighter takes a lot of his opponent's body punches on his arms and Harold's were becoming sore, bruised and heavy. The advantage Hill held in youth and fitness was beginning to tell.

Instinctively, Harold was aware that Hill must also be tiring and in pain and if he could hang on a little longer, he could still beat him. He sensed that Hill's concentration was dwindling.

The Tomato Fight

In an instant, he reverted to an old favourite trick. He threw his left arm almost at ninety degrees to his left side and followed the arc of his fist with darting eyes as he did so. Hill fell for the trap. Almost as if he was hypnotised, his eyes followed the path of his opponent's. The Englishman learned a lesson in street fighting in that instant. Harold measured his momentarily distracted foe and delivered a right cross with all of the force and will that he could dredge up from within. He threw the punch from close to his chest, harnessing all of the strength in his shoulder and upper body, just as he'd been taught so long ago. Mick Dixon would've been proud.

Sssnap!

It caught Hill flush on the point of his jaw, the angle just below his left ear. His eyes glazed over, his shoulders slumped and his guard dropped slightly. Harold knew that his moment had come.

By deflecting his gaze – and his concentration – from Harold, Hill had made a disastrous error. 'If you slew, you blue,' Harold murmured, happy that an old chestnut had roasted so deliciously. He followed up the right cross with his favourite combination, a left rip and hook, then a right uppercut and as many blows as he had left in him, one after another, delivered with all of his diminishing strength. They were unanswered.

Hill had no way of knowing it, but some of the accumulated debts that he was now settling were not ones that he had been responsible for. Some belonged to the nuns, quite a few to the coppers and to the rapists. Hill had to pay his own as well, of course – and he did, his receipt signed with a simple, succinct message: 'Don't touch my family.'

Hill crumpled, all but unconscious, against the wall of the shopfront, to the approving roars of the men in the crowd watching. They'd witnessed plenty of street fights before but few of this calibre.

'Come on, you pommie dog. Get up.' Harold's muted challenge to continue was forthright but delivered with more bravado than it probably should have been. He'd spent it all. There was nothing left.

'No . . . no,' surrendered Hill meekly, quietly, almost incoherently, spitting blood. His nose and cheekbone were smashed. 'I'm . . . gone.'

Harold drew back, stood above the vanquished Englishman for a moment and then turned to find his family. Young Harold was as excited as he'd ever been in his life.

'Good on ya, Dad. Jeez, that was good. You beat 'im, didn' ya?'

Harold barely had the energy to answer. 'Yeah, son, I s'pose I did.'

Ignoring the slaps on the back from the local cheer squadron, Harold gathered together his clan. Tony was silent – he held Diane securely, in a familiar pose, astride his hip. He'd covered her eyes with his free hand during the fight. She had no need to witness any of it. He held firm opinions – and still does now – about not resorting to violence to resolve issues. He was a mentally strong boy with more mature, rigid value systems than most others of his age – and he never would resile from his duty to express them when the occasion arose.

He might never come to appreciate the reasoning behind what his father had just felt compelled to do. He, like the other children, had no perception of the creed of the mean streets that Harold knew so well and had lived so much of his life by. He'd planned it this way – so that at least while they were under his protection, his kids would never need to know about such things.

John, too, had been clinging to his brother, aghast and weeping with fright. 'Did he hurt you, Dad?' he asked his father, between sobs.

Harold lied: 'No, no, John, don't worry, I'm all right.' He placed a comforting, reassuring – though quivering – arm around John's shoulders and then took Diane from Tony's arms. 'Thanks, Tony,' he said. 'You're a good boy.'

A calmer Ronald was already sitting on the steps as they entered the gate at the front of the house. He'd been granted a special gift: the ability to ignore, even dismiss from his consciousness, unpleasant or awkward situations. He had a positive and non-judgmental, guileless and always easygoing outlook on life. His detachment was a nuisance to Dora, though. Whenever she took her brood on an outing, one of her initial instructions was always to Ronald. She would indicate a meeting point for him to return to when, inevitably and despite her best efforts, he became lost. 'Where's Ronald?' was an oft-repeated phrase in the family. There always seemed to be a tree that needed to be climbed, a fence to jump over or a wall to jump from that were invisible to others' eyes. He would eventually turn up, sometimes with scrapes and scratches from some little misadventure, but safe and reasonably sound nonetheless.

Dora spent the rest of the evening feeding the family and tending to Harold's injuries. He had escaped with all of his teeth intact but plenty of bruises to his body and nicks and cuts to his face and hands. Much of the skin was gone from his knuckles. She bathed them in salty water, then used cotton wool to dab them with salve. Harold enjoyed the attention. It was rare that he'd ever had someone to look after him following a fight. His mind was cast back to that night in the Valley when he'd been attacked by Clark and Muller, then nursed by Annie and Dora afterwards.

Few altercations had been as tough for him or had taken such a toll on his body as this one had. His wife was full of love and appreciation for his actions. It wouldn't have mattered whether he had won the fight or lost it. She still would've felt the same way. It was the first time that he'd ever been called upon to defend her honour and she was proud of him, although unprepared for the exhilaration that it afforded her. The sheer strength and toughness of his actions that night simply thrilled her. At that moment, she was more in love with him than she had ever been.

Young Harold couldn't get to sleep for hours. He couldn't wait to get to school at St James's to tell his mates all about it. Harold the elder had the opposite experience: he was exhausted and slept soundly. But, like his first-born, he too had some urgent business planned for the morning.

As soon as he awoke, Harold pulled on the singlet that he'd been wearing the day before and his trousers, rolling up the cuffs to shin height. Barefoot, he headed out the front door and down the steps. Dora hurried after him, instructing Tony to look after the younger children for her. Their eldest son was quick to follow her.

'Harold, what are you doing? Where are you going?' she called to her husband.

He said nothing. He walked to the front of Hill's shop, stood at the doorway and again rapped his knuckles on the window. The action stung. He tried to make a fist. The abraded skin stretched and it hurt, a lot. Having attracted Hill's attention, he signalled for him to come out and face him again.

Hill couldn't believe his eyes. He wasn't going anywhere near Fingleton, that was for sure. 'No, no more,' he shouted, ducking his battered head down below the shop counter to hide from his sight.

'Well, you've gotta come out sometime,' Harold called back. 'And I'll be here waitin' for you when you do.'

Hill put his business on the market and he and his family were gone within the week.

Harold would often say: 'It's the backup that beats 'em, son.'

23

The Betrayal

A moment in time that may make us unhappy forever

John Gay (1685–1732), *The Beggar's Opera*

With the disbanding of the Valley All Whites Football Club in 1953, the weekly gatherings at the Fingleton family home during football season were no more, somewhat to Dora's relief. Preparing food and cleaning up afterwards was time-consuming and tedious, even though the family had usually tackled it together.

Harold and Dora's social life now revolved around going to the pictures or the occasional dance – still Dora's favourite pastime and still at the Railway Institute Hall – on Friday nights. The hall and the city theatres were all within comfortable walking distance of their house and they enjoyed walking rather than taking the short bus ride.

Their other great love was the card evenings they held most Saturdays and some Sundays with a few close friends, playing games of rickety Kate, euchre, rummy or whist. Tommy was always there, of course. He was still a much-loved and welcome visitor at their place and always called in on Sunday evening for dinner. He was particularly popular with the children, because he never arrived without a bag of chocolates for them to share. Irish and Edie Radley and Brickie and Maggie Farrell came, too, along with more recent additions to their circle of friends, Jim and Chrissie Unwin, and Bill and Flo Croker.

Jim Unwin was a retired boxer who worked on the wharves with Harold and Bill. Harold often described Jim as 'a very dangerous man', sometimes to his face. It was a private joke that made both of them chuckle. Jim had an identical twin brother named Ernie who was a more accomplished boxer than Jim; in fact, he had an unbeaten record, of which Jim was justifiably jealous. They were descended from the North American Algonquin Cree Indian tribe and were fearless, true warriors themselves. They were full of rampant but controlled aggression and if things were quiet, they'd fight each other – no punches pulled – just for fun. Once, when Jim was short of money, he took a fight in Ernie's name, without his knowledge. The bloke he fought was a much better boxer but Jim fluked his opponent with a hard right and knocked him out. When

Ernie found out, he was livid. He told Jim, 'Just as well you never spoilt my record, otherwise I'd have spoilt your face.' Chrissie was a tall, very slender, pretty woman with a wicked grin. When she smiled, her eyes glistened and you couldn't help but smile with her. She was the one upon whom Dora most often called to sit with her children whenever she and Harold went out for the evening. You could entrust your very life to Chrissie.

William Harrington Croker had dabbled in the mire of the criminal underworld as a younger man but had been straight for years now, ever since he had succumbed to the charms and the calming influence of Florence, a sweet but strong, capable woman who had been a hospital matron before she met Bill. Dark and oily skinned, with cruel-looking, narrow eyes, Bill sported a long, wide, ugly scar that ran from his ear to his chin, on the right side of his face. It was the result of a knife fight. It looked as if it had healed without stitching. Because of his looks, the younger Fingleton children feared Bill – quite unreasonably as it so happened, because he was extremely gentle with kids.

Bill had once been shot in the stomach. His life was saved only because a famous doctor from Chicago who had developed a stomach surgery technique for repairing bullet wounds was visiting Australia at the time on a lecture tour and performed the operation on him. Many a felon was said to owe his life to this doctor's expertise. When the police had gone to see Bill in the hospital to ask him to identify the shooter, Bill laughed in their faces and abused them for having the temerity to ask. He would never, ever give information to the police. If and when he had his chance, he would square his own ledger. His assailant was killed some time later. Bill swore that he'd had nothing to do with it and blamed it on the police. He was never charged over the killing.

There was one other regular, Alan Wilson, a bachelor who had become friendly with Harold while also working on the wharf. Alan was a few years younger than the rest of them and sought Harold's approval on most issues. Keen to impress Harold with tales of his toughness, Alan skited about the regular victories that he said he'd won in bar fights around the city. Harold humoured the bloke and listened, seemingly intently, through each and every boring detail. He'd always known that really tough people don't have to and choose not to, brag about their toughness. Their taciturnity is what makes them all the more dangerous, for it gives them the advantage of the element of surprise.

A tall, rather suave fellow, Alan always wore a suit and fancied himself as the answer to every woman's romantic dreams. He teased and flirted with Dora constantly but she and Harold both considered him harmless. Occasionally he would bring his latest female conquest along for the evening. His friends never questioned Alan's often less than tasteful choice of female company. The women came and went at a rate of about one every couple of weeks – causing Dora to mention to her husband that Alan might not be the great lover that he considered himself to be. Alan and his various women were made to feel welcome, however, at the Fingleton house.

And then came an unexpected event in their social life one Saturday evening in late November 1953, one that was to prove momentous in the lives of Harold and Dora. It would test the bonds of, and define, their marriage for some years to come.

Just as Harold and Dora were cleaning up after dinner, Irish and Edie arrived, having walked from their home a couple of blocks up from the Fingletons'. Irish had become quite wealthy, having successfully operated a number of starting-price betting shops in the near-city suburbs. Edie was prone to overdress and wear far too much makeup and jewellery. Dora and she were chatting in the lounge room while Irish and Harold sat on the back verandah having a smoke and enjoying the late-spring breeze. Dora answered a knock at the front door and welcomed in Alan and his newest girlfriend. They walked down the hallway into the lounge, just as Harold entered from the verandah. Alan proudly introduced his lady to the company. Each was more impressed than they normally would have been. It was impossible not to be taken with the woman's beauty. The ladies admired the expensive-looking, fashionable cotton frock that fell gracefully about a svelte and shapely figure.

'Good evenin', everyone. I'd like youse all to meet Cathy.'

'Hello, Cathy. I'm Edie.'

'Nice to meet you, Cathy. I'm Dora.'

'My name's Jack, Cathy. Call me Irish. How are ya?'

Harold was speechless, not that anyone would think anything of that. He was often reticent when it came to meeting one of Alan's lady friends, or any woman for that matter.

'Jesus Christ …' he muttered beneath his breath. He hoped that nobody would notice the heat that he could feel welling in his face. His ears felt hot and were ringing.

It was Cathy Churchill.

Their eyes met briefly. Harold nodded his acknowledgment then quickly cast his glance away. His mind was a tempest but he tried to act as normally as possible, as if she was unknown to him. Cathy did the same in return.

Harold had never mentioned Cathy's name to Dora. When they discussed the years that he had spent estranged from her in Sydney, he had told her that he'd been involved with a woman and had become 'pretty wrapped in her'. Dora knew that he and the woman had lived together but didn't know what she'd done for a living, what she looked like or anything else about her. When Dora had asked why their relationship had ended, Harold said that when he had been gaoled for consorting, she'd left him and he hadn't heard from her since.

Knowing nothing about cards, Cathy didn't join in the game and opted to sit quietly next to Alan, occasionally getting up to prepare a cup of tea, saving Dora the trouble. The guests would all have preferred an alcoholic drink, yet in deference to Harold – but never at his insistence – they refrained from drinking when they were at the Fingletons.

Dora was charmed by the new arrival. She was personable, chatty, easy to like. While they were preparing some supper, she asked Cathy if she'd been married. Cathy told her that she had been and was the mother of a seven-year-old girl. When her marriage had failed, she'd moved from Sydney to Brisbane to begin a new life. Dora was keen to know more about Cathy's child. She loved to talk about children, especially her own. The child was named Donna, Cathy informed her, and she was enrolled at St Stephen's Convent School for the new school year, beginning the following February. Dora thought it a lovely coincidence that she would be going to the same school as her younger ones and would be in Diane's class.

The card evening finished earlier than it usually would. It was common for them to play well into the early hours or at least until a heated, though always harmless, argument broke out. This night, though, Harold complained of one of his regular migraines and retired to bed.

Before she left, Dora invited Cathy to call over and bring Donna with her during the daytime, to play with her kids. She was concerned that the little girl wouldn't have had a chance to make any friends in the brief time that she and her mother had been in Brisbane.

During the next few weeks, Cathy and her daughter became regular visitors. The children played happily together and Cathy was a good conversationalist. Dora enjoyed her company immensely and loved the way that she dressed and always looked so beautiful. She would've liked to have been able to afford to do the same but knew she never would. It didn't bother her, though, because she was married to the man she loved, had a healthy band of children and her life was happy enough. She could ask for little more, the way she saw it.

Harold was aware that his wife was becoming more enamoured of Cathy with each visit. Dora spoke of her constantly – about their conversations, the clothes that she had worn on her last visit, how gorgeous little Donna was. He had so far managed to avoid contact with Cathy, who visited only when he was on day shift. He was biding his time for the chance to see her alone and warn her off. His life was the best it had ever been.

One day he was at home, resting for a midnight-to-dawn shift. He hated those shifts. Even during summer, the wind off the river could blow a chill through him in the early morning hours. He would spend the week of midnight shifts in a state of progressive rancour. Because he found great difficulty in sleeping during the daylight hours, by the end of the working week, his nerves would be frazzled, his temper touchy. Dora and the kids learned to tread a little more quietly during those weeks. For the kids especially, bursting with rampant energy and by now on school holidays, it wasn't easy.

For once, Harold had slipped into a light, fairly restful state of slumber. There was a knock at the front door. He ignored it. The caller knocked again. He called for Dora to answer it. There was no response. He assumed that she must have stepped out. When the visitor knocked yet again, he sighed deeply and got up to investigate. It might be a problem with one of the kids. 'Probably that bloody Harold, or Ronald,' he muttered. Ronald was always hurting himself somehow. Hadn't he tried to race a car when crossing the street one day and been bowled over? Thank Christ he wasn't hurt.

Harold opened the door. Cathy stood before him.

'Dora's not here, Cathy, but come in anyway. I've been waitin' for the chance to talk to you.'

Cathy followed him into the lounge room. He didn't invite her to sit. What he had to say wouldn't take long.

'Thanks, Harold, but I know Dora's not here,' Cathy said. 'She told me the other day she had to go to the endowment office today. I've been waiting for a chance to talk to you, too.'

'Yeah? What about?'

She knew that the direct approach was the best method to use with him. He'd never been one to waste words. She told him that she'd been surprised and disappointed that he hadn't tried to see her privately before this. 'I'll tell you straight, Harold. I want you back. I still love you.'

He shook his head. 'What bull – '

'Please let me finish, Harold. I've thought about nothing else for the past couple of years. I've got a beautiful little girl who needs a father. I've saved up lots of money. We could move back to Sydney or up north and start afresh, couldn't we?'

By now she had moved close to him. He didn't back away from her. The years had been kind to her. Indeed, she was even more beautiful now than he had remembered. She smelt so good – her familiar scent filled his nostrils and was sweet, alluring, difficult to resist. It would've been so easy to take advantage of her willingness, if only this once, and indulge himself.

She reached out to him, clutched his hands in hers and pushed herself against his body. His head was swimming with feelings of sexual desire the like of which he hadn't experienced in a long time, his body thrilling to her touch, her closeness irresistible. They kissed. He knew that what he was doing could lead to no good. He filled his arms with the sensuous, lithe body that he now craved.

Neither heard the latch on the lattice back door as it was lifted. Dora had forgotten to take the paperwork she needed to collect their child endowment, the subsidy the government provided to parents, and she would have to go back the next day. She'd collected some washing from the clothesline in the back yard on her way in. By the time Harold and Cathy had become aware of her presence, she was standing, riveted to the spot in shock, at the door of the lounge room. Dora calmly placed the basket of laundry on the small table on the verandah.

'Well, isn't this lovely. Are you two enjoying yourselves?' Her anger was muted, controlled for the time being.

The couple disengaged from their embrace. Red-faced and stuttering with embarrassment, Harold attempted to think of something to say. He failed.

'Dora, I –' began Cathy.

'Don't say anything, Cathy,' said Dora firmly, quietly, her determination utterly unmistakable. 'I think you should just get out of my house. Harold, if you want to, you can go with her.'

'I'm sorry, Dora,' muttered Cathy.

'I know you are, Cathy. Sorry you got caught. Just get out, please – now! Well, Harold, are you going, too?'

His response was a brief, sheepish: 'No, Dora, I'm not – I'll stay – I can explain this.'

'It'll need to be good. Well, Cathy, what are you waiting for?'

Cathy gathered her handbag from the lounge-room table and in an instant, relieved not to have to explain herself, was gone. They would never see her or hear from her again.

Dora wouldn't waste the tears that welled in her eyes. Tears didn't affect her husband, never had. Her chest seemed fit to explode with anger. But it was best for the moment to remain calm, resolute, in control. She had learned much over the years about dealing with Harold Fingleton.

'Well, Harold, what've you got to say? How could you do this to me, to the kids – and in our own house? How –'

Harold interrupted her. 'Let's sit down, Dora. This'll take a while.' He attempted to appear as calm as possible.

'You sit down if you want to. I'm right where I am.' Her ire was such that she preferred to be able to move about. She felt as if she wanted to hit him or throw something at him.

Harold made his way to the kitchen. 'Do you want a cup of tea?'

'Bugger the bloody tea, Harold! Just start talking if you've got something to say.'

He pulled one of the chairs out from the kitchen table and sat. 'Do you remember me tellin' you about the sheila I got tied up with in Sydney?'

'Yes, of course.'

'Well, it was Cathy.'

'Cathy!' Dora was shocked. 'What . . . how . . .'

'Let me tell you the lot. No point in havin' any secrets now.'

Dora sat in silence as he told her of the relationship that he and Cathy had shared, how long they had been together, his part in finding customers for her, the way it had all ended. Another woman might have been shocked but it was of no consequence to Dora that Harold had been associated with a prostitute. While he had been away, his life was his to lead.

'I haven't got a clue how she found me,' he went on. 'I don't suppose it would've been that hard. She knew where I used to knock about up here. I told her a lot about meself. I s'pose she just got herself and her kid up here and started askin' questions around the Valley. She's a smart bastard.' His voice was steady. There was no trace of pleading or feeling sorry for himself – he was simply quiet, honest, forthright.

Dora knew that everything he was telling her was true. It simply had to be. Their future lives together depended upon it. 'Yes,' she added in reply. 'Smart like a bloody rat.'

'Look, Dora, I never planned any of what just happened. She just showed up today, knowin' you were out. She wanted me to go away with her.'

'And?'

He shook his head slowly from side to side. 'No way in the bloody world. That would never have happened. I wouldn't want to leave me kids, or you.'

Dora, who had calmed down somewhat, took a deep breath – the first she'd been aware of for some minutes. She had no idea whether she was feeling any better or not. It would take some time for her to digest it all, make some decisions. She looked up at the kitchen clock and realised that it was now late afternoon. 'You'd better go and get some rest if you have to leave at eleven,' she said quietly.

'Right.' He rose and left the room, reaching out to touch her hand as he passed by her.

'Don't you dare touch me, Harold. You make me sick. Just leave me alone and don't be too sure that we'll all be here when you come home in the morning.'

Harold was fairly confident that her threat was merely a scare tactic. She had no money of her own and there was nowhere for her to go where he would not quickly find her. 'I'm sorry, Dora' was all he had to offer. There was no response and he headed for the bedroom to get some rest if he could.

It would be easier for them both that he was working tonight, he thought. By the time morning arrived, their tensions may have eased a little – at least, that was what he hoped.

24

Little Fishes

The world may be divided into those who take it or leave it and those who split the difference

Father Ronald Knox (1888–1957)

The tension between Harold and Dora gradually did ease but not for several months. Harold was banished to a small single bed on the back verandah. Dora sometimes could not bring herself to cook for him and he wished he'd learned some kitchen skills at some stage in his life – the two boiled eggs and toast that he occasionally prepared for himself became less and less palatable as time wore on. He would've loved to have been able to express to Dora, in a manner satisfying to her, his regret over the incident. He simply struggled to put into words his true feelings. He felt anger at his weakness in the face of Cathy's advances. He wondered if perhaps he'd simply been flattered that he was still attractive to another woman.

Dora seemed to have lost some of her passion for life. One of her greatest assets, her eternal good humour and optimism – present during even the most difficult times, such as when one of the children was sick – had gone. He hoped he'd be able to regain her confidence in time and was determined to do so. As much as he was assured of her love for him, he knew he must never test it in such a way again. He realised that he was a long way from being the ideal husband and Dora deserved so much better. He realised also that the best he could do was to continue to work hard to provide for her and their kids and hope that time would work its sorcery. No one could know better than he how fortune had smiled upon him in giving him his family, the gift that he treasured so much. Only a complete fool would put it all at risk again.

One absolute could never be denied or challenged: that was Harold and Dora's devotion to their children. The children were their greatest achievement, more than they could have dared to hope for. Feeding, protecting and educating them became the nucleus around which their universe revolved. The five kids were the thread that knitted the marriage together, that bound and secured it, and they would become all that Harold and Dora lived for.

Young Harold was showing great promise as a footballer at school, much to his father's delight. Harold wanted to have at least one footballer in the family. Happiest when he was giving his boys the benefit of his knowledge of the game, he regularly spent hours with them practising in the back yard or at one of the local parks. His eldest had the talent and the toughness to make it in the game and wouldn't lack for expertise in any of its finer points.

Harold would often take the kids for a swim at the local baths and had told Dora one day, 'They can all swim like little fishes.' He enrolled them as members of the Fortitude Valley Amateur Swimming Club and they competed there every Wednesday night, with success. Now it was time, he reckoned, for them to start training a little more seriously. It would be good for their health and, as he'd always contended, would 'keep 'em busy – out of trouble'. He knew that Tony, in particular, needed to strengthen up. The several illnesses that he'd suffered over the years were mostly not serious but he was thinner than the rest of the boys and tough exercise could be especially beneficial to him.

Dora would often watch them from the front verandah as they crossed Boundary Street on their way to the pool for twice-daily training sessions, each carrying their swimming costume and towel. Ronald and young Harold, ever the competitors, would race ahead to be first into the water. The rest would hold their collective breaths until those two had made it safely to the opposite footpath. Tony took it upon himself to look after Diane and would take her hand in his and guide her safely all of the way. John, lazy and unenthusiastic about the boredom of the hard work ahead, invariably brought up the rear.

Dora could've burst with pride for her brood but, invariably, her last glance fell upon the square shoulders of her husband. She would never fully come to terms with what had happened on that dreadful day but it would gradually fade in importance beneath the weight of all the considerations involved in providing a safe and healthy life for their children. Harold had proven his mettle in many ways in the months since then. It was not in his nature to yield to the expectations of others and she was full of admiration for him that he had managed to fulfil, for the most part, the commitments that he'd undertaken to uphold when they married. She knew that the future would hold many highs and lows – some bliss and some turmoil – and that he probably would never, ever be tamed completely. She was determined, though, that her own inner strength and the depth of her love for him and their children would see them through.

In Conclusion

Do not go gentle into that good night,
Old age should burn and rage at close of day;
Rage, rage against the dying of the light.

Dylan Thomas (1914–53)

My mother was right: her love and dedication, and my father's, not only saw us through good times and bad, it gave us the kind of opportunities in life they could only have dreamed of.

Harold the younger worked as a bricklayer. He played first-grade football in Brisbane for several years as a young man. He fought his own grand battle with alcohol for thirty-five years, eventually declaring himself triumphant. He suffered the pain of a failed marriage but he and his son, Marc, remain close friends, travelling extensively together.

He met Val, with whom he shared a wonderful and loving relationship that lasted two decades until her premature death from multiple sclerosis in 2007. Harold devoted himself to her gentle care until the sad and harrowing end. He has not taken a drink for nearly twenty years and shares a love of, and many rounds of, golf with Ron and Diane. Both Harold and Ron play off low handicaps. Diane has only recently converted to the game and is a rapid improver.

Tony's career can best be described as brilliant. After selection in the Australian swimming team, he represented his country with distinction at the 1962 Perth Commonwealth Games, winning a silver medal. He applied for and was granted a scholarship to study at Harvard University. He graduated with a degree in economics and business administration in 1967 and married Pamela Wolcott, an executive secretary at Radcliffe College and a member of a very traditional New England banking family based in Boston. Tony has lived and worked successfully as a writer and film producer in New York since 1968 and is the father of two girls, Samantha and Priscilla, and the doting grandfather of another three – Abigail, Rosie and Avery. He has co-written and co-produced various feature films, including *Drop Dead Fred* and *Swimming Upstream*, his depiction of his somewhat unhappy relationship with our father. He and Pamela live very comfortably, on Manhattan's exclusive Upper East Side.

In Conclusion

Despite desperate overtures from the Christian Brothers at St Joseph's College, Gregory Terrace, where our parents had organised study scholarships for Tony, Ronald and me, I refused to see my secondary education through to its conclusion. Impatient and eager for some independence, I started my working life as a junior clerk with the Bank of New South Wales during the summer of my eighteenth year. It would be the first of many, varied mini-careers, from road-paving contractor to croupier, taxi driver to licensed bookmaker, to name but a few. I achieved above-average success at state and national levels as a pool and surf swimmer. I married young, that union ill-fated and brief but producing a fine son, Grant. Then I met and fell in love with kind, gentle, sweet Sylvia. We live in Sydney and in January 2011 celebrated the fortieth anniversary of our extraordinarily happy marriage.

Ronald has experienced a charmed and mostly happy existence. He was a brilliant and gifted natural athlete, representing his state in several sports, never taking any one of them very seriously, apart from his great love, water polo. He was once eloquently described by Tony as going through life 'on roller skates'. Ron has married twice and had three children, Nathan, Sarah and Camille, each of whom are now parents themselves. Eventually he settled into a strong relationship with Lyn, his partner. He runs a small, successful coffee machine business and, with his generally kind, easygoing disposition, remains the middleman among his siblings. Each of us, over the years, has experienced temporary personality clashes with one or more of the rest, following the tradition of most well-ordered families. Ron's absolute loyalty to his family is one of his worthiest and most undeniable attributes.

Diane travelled extensively as a young woman and worked for a number of years in London and New York. After she returned to Australia, she was appointed to the staff of the serving federal treasurer, Bill Hayden.

Over time, Diane became more and more conscious of the plight of the needier elements of society. She came to recognise the need to provide affordable and capable legal representation to the less fortunate. To this end, and with strong encouragement from Hayden, she studied law, working to pay her way through university. Soon after graduation, although courted keenly by several legal firms and working briefly for one, she assisted in the foundation of a legal aid service. She won acclaim for her untiring efforts on behalf of abused women and children and for her work on Aboriginal issues and consumer affairs. She eventually married a solicitor named John McGrath, the love of her life, and was appointed to the magistracy, progressing rapidly to the position of chief magistrate. She played a major role in the establishment of the highly successful Murri Court in Queensland.

In Conclusion

Tragically, in 2002, Diane was unfairly accused and convicted of intimidating a witness, and was imprisoned. Her conviction was quashed by the High Court of Australia and she was again appointed as a magistrate. Her amazing fight for justice and recovery from her tribulations demonstrated her immense fortitude. She tells her story in her excellent book *Nothing To Do With Justice*. Diane is now happily retired, although she remains in high demand for lectures and speeches.

*

Unfortunately, Dad's alcoholism became a major problem for him and the rest of us from the mid-1950s onwards. His resolve weakened after nineteen years of tenaciously defying his urge to drink. The real cause of his breakdown remains a mystery to us all; it could have been one of so many things.

I often wondered if he thought his job as protector and provider was largely accomplished by then. Perhaps it was something as simple as a mid-life crisis. Certainly, the timing was right. It's normal for a man's physical strength to show initial, distinct signs of diminishing at this point in his life. For a man of his virility and strength of body and will, such a loss might've been harder to cope with for him than most. Or was it the demons of his past revisiting and exerting influences impossible for him to resist any longer? Most likely, it was the latter but I don't have the answers, to this day.

He did manage at times to gather himself up and dry out but after a while, his will would collapse and another binge would begin. Dealing with the dreadful expectation of these on again, off again phases became a dominant feature of our lives, especially during our teenage years.

My mother had always hoped that Dad would mellow as he aged but instead, he became more moodily morose and depressive. At the lowest ebb of his depression, he subjected her and at times us, his children, to mentally scarring verbal abuse. Although he never physically harmed Mum, his irate, threatening behaviour finally reached a saturation point for her. It simply wore her out and after thirty-five years of marriage, they separated, although they did not divorce.

Dora at first went and stayed with Diane at Highgate Hill, an inner-city southern suburb of Brisbane. Dad, who had retired from work on the wharves two years previously, lived alone in a gloomy bedsitter not far away, in Hill End. He became friends with a young fellow named Selwyn Keid, who lived across the laneway with his middle-aged, wealthy, widowed mother, in a spacious, expensively furnished house. Selwyn was twenty-four but already was a confirmed alcoholic and a compulsive, inveterate gambler. My father was pleased to have the company of the young man to drink with at the hotel

In Conclusion

and to accompany him safely home at night. Before long, Selwyn had begun inviting him into his home for some breakfast or a cup of tea before they'd head off to the pub. Dad would happily accept, always aware that it would keep him going for the day if he had some food in his stomach. Mrs Keid was a gracious, kind and cultured woman who seemingly felt sorry for my father and made him welcome.

One morning Dad was awakened from a semi-comatose, drunken slumber by a loud knock at the door. Groggily, garbed only in pyjama pants and singlet, he arose to open it and was confronted by the sight of two men in shirtsleeves and ties. He knew instantly, without inquiry, that they were policemen.

They wished to ask him a few questions. Did he know Mrs Keid from across the way? Yeah. Had he recently been in her house? Yeah. When? 'Yesterd'y mornin,' he answered. And was Mrs Keid alive the last time he had seen her?

Jesus! The question shocked him to his core. His grog-addled brain all but exploded within his skull. This was nice. Mrs Keid was dead. They must've decided that she'd been murdered or they wouldn't have been asking him questions. With his violent criminal record from his early days, they'd fit him for the crime without raising a sweat. He was gone.

The two officers questioned him for thirty minutes or so and he answered them directly – careful, as he always had been, not to give away anything superfluous. He wouldn't be giving anyone else up, despite his own precarious position. Dad remained outwardly calm and composed, although within, he was in turmoil and had already begun mapping out the rest of his days as a prisoner back at Boggo Road.

When they'd finished with him, the policeman calmly took their leave, telling him that he had nothing to worry about. He was stunned with relief. They'd decided, with the benefit of their training and experience with criminals, that my father was innocent of any wrongdoing in this case. Having established that fact, it was clear to them who the guilty party probably was. It would be the person who had called them to his home and then directed them to the old drunkard's door.

Selwyn Keid was charged with, and found guilty of, the murder of his mother. He had strangled her to death. Dad felt that Keid had planned the entire exercise well, but not well enough, and that he was meant to be the scapegoat. Keid would have to forego the massive inheritance that he'd planned to get his hands on much earlier than he was entitled to. He received a life sentence and served about sixteen years before being released. His defence counsel during his trial was one John Maxwell McGrath, the same John McGrath who would meet and marry Diane several years hence.

Not long after that sordid event took place, Dad awoke one morning and thought that he was about to die, so sick did he feel from the effects of his latest binge. He made up his

In Conclusion

mind to stop drinking once and for all, then and there. This time, it was for good. He moved into a Housing Commission flat at New Farm. Mum had a Housing Commission flat in Zillmere, in the northern suburbs of Brisbane, about fifteen kilometres away from New Farm.

Over the next half-dozen years, my father and mother spent many of their daylight hours together. She'd prepare and bring him a meal to his place or he would catch public transport to hers at Zillmere. She told me that whenever he left to go home, she would always watch him go.

He'd take a short cut across an adjacent vacant paddock on his way to the railway station. One day as he walked through the paddock, he was attacked by a pair of nesting magpies. His reaction was typical: he stood there and threw slaps and punches at the darting, pecking birds, before realising how ridiculous he must have looked. He quickly glanced back towards Mum, to find her in fits of laughter. He himself burst out laughing and then gave her a brief shadow-sparring exhibition and a deep bow before continuing jauntily on his way. When he reached the final corner from which they could still see each other, as always, he turned her way again so they could exchange a wave.

She told me that in that moment of fun, she recalled with clarity the young show-off with whom she had fallen so deeply in love all of those years before. He never had changed very much, really, Mum assured me, and neither had she.

She told me what I'd always chosen to believe: that she still cared deeply for my father. She knew me well, as she did all of her children. Each needed comfort and consolation in differing ways and she was the ultimate expert in providing it.

My dad survived his old mate Tommy Thurman, who virtually drank himself to death, aged seventy, lonely except for Harold's undying friendship. Mum and Dad laid Tom to rest in a burial plot close to Maggie's, at Toowong Cemetery.

Knobby Clark and my dad were never likely to become friends. On Dad's seventieth birthday, in January 1979, I took him on one of our regular sporting outings, to a cricket match at the Gabba. I had heard a lot about the angst between my father and Clark as young men, so when they unexpectedly bumped into each other that day, I was bemused to see them greet each other rather warmly and spend the next couple of hours sitting together.

They watched the cricket and amicably discussed their lives and their children's achievements. It was as if two old warriors had come to terms with their differences – and to me, it was fascinating and touching. Perhaps peace, finally, had been declared. But as the former copper stood to leave, Dad deftly removed Knobby's wallet from his back pocket, nudging me as he did so, to draw my attention to what he was doing. He waited until Clark had reached the end of the row and begun to make his way up the grandstand steps before he called after him.

In Conclusion

Holding the wallet aloft between thumb and forefinger, he said, a wide grin across his face, 'Knobby, did you lose this?'

Clark knew he hadn't lost it. Red-faced, he returned to retrieve his property. As he took it from Dad's grasp, he whispered, 'Fingleton, you bastard. You're incorrigible.'

My father nodded and replied, 'Yeah, Knobby, I probably am.'

Clark died a couple of years later, well into his eighties. His funeral cortege was large and he was honoured by speeches from various police dignitaries. My father chose not to attend.

Annie Milner, my maternal grandmother, went to Bowen, in north Queensland, to live and to care for Jock and his two children, Ann and Brian, in 1951. Uncle Jock and Aunty Winifred had decided to abort her third pregnancy, but fell victim to a charlatan. Winifred died from the aftereffects of the botched procedure. Jock suffered a fatal heart seizure in his late fifties, while Annie passed away soon after from natural causes, aged eighty. She and my mother had continued to conduct a cool, strained relationship. For Mum, Annie's occasional visits to Brisbane with the two children for Christmas and school holidays were more than sufficient contact. There was an air of tension during each visit.

Mollie, my dad's eldest sister, outlived her beloved Lucy by nearly ten years. Then she suffered a broken hip in a fall while taking a shower. She was hospitalised and operated upon successfully but, unable to move about, she developed pneumonia and died. Mollie was ninety-seven years old and had witnessed the demise of all of her siblings.

Dad passed away, having suffered with emphysema and lung cancer, in August, 1985. Diane and I had to inform him at the end that there was nothing further that the medical staff could do for him. He was to be removed from the Royal Brisbane, where he'd been undergoing treatment, to the hospice at Mount Olivet.

His response was an almost whispered, breathless, 'Ah well, that's it then, eh.'

In that moment, I thought that I detected the dropping of his guard. I saw the merest trace of an unfamiliar look of dread, perhaps even fear, in his fading, now almost grey, eyes. I imagined that it was the same look that might have appeared on a defiant countenance on the day, a long time ago, when a little boy had been confronted with the news that he was to be removed from his mother's care to an unknown fate at St Vincent's Orphanage. The larrikin died two days later.

Mum was diagnosed with lymphatic cancer in October 1988, having originally entered hospital for a gall bladder operation. She passed away peacefully, a little over three years after Dad had gone. She was surrounded by the only other people who had ever mattered to her – her beloved and devoted family.

About the author

John Fingleton was born in Brisbane in 1943, the third in a family of five to Harold and Dora. In 1960 he left school to pursue a career in banking. He quickly became bored with that and shifted from job to job until he realised he would never be happy working for anyone else. For the past 35 years, he has largely been self-employed, mostly in transport.

Like his siblings, John excelled at swimming, winning twelve medals at national swimming and surf lifesaving championships between 1960 and 1964 as well as multiple awards at school and state level along the way.

The Australian film *Swimming Upstream*, written and co-produced by his brother, Tony, directed by Russell Mulcahy and starring Geoffrey Rush, became the impetus for the writing of *Surviving Maggie*, his first book.

John lives in Sydney with his wife of 40 years, Sylvia.

Acknowledgements

Past inmates of St Vincent's, Nudgee Orphanage –
For the willing and invaluable assistance they provided in the research for this book

Queensland Government Department of Families

New South Wales Police Business Services

Care Leavers of Australia Network – CLAN – Bankstown, NSW